BEHIND THE LINE

A Story of College Life and Football

RALPH HENRY BARBOUR

1st WORLD
LIBRARY
Literary Society

Behind the Line

Ralph Henry Barbour

© 1st World Library, 2006
PO Box 2211
Fairfield, IA 52556
www.1stworldlibrary.com
First Edition

LCCN: 2006935356

Softcover ISBN: 1-4218-2501-5
Hardcover ISBN: 1-4218-2401-9
eBook ISBN: 1-4218-2601-1

Purchase "*Behind the Line*"
as a traditional bound book at:
www.1stWorldLibrary.com/purchase.asp?ISBN=1-4218-2501-5

1st World Library Literary Society

Giving Back to the World

"If you want to work on the core problem, it's early school literacy."

- James Barksdale, former CEO of Netscape

"No skill is more crucial to the future of a child, or to a democratic and prosperous society, than literacy."

- Los Angeles Times

Literacy... means far more than learning how to read and write... The aim is to transmit... knowledge and promote social participation."

- UNESCO

"Literacy is not a luxury, it is a right and a responsibility. If our world is to meet the challenges of the twenty-first century we must harness the energy and creativity of all our citizens."

- President Bill Clinton

"Parents should be encouraged to read to their children, and teachers should be equipped with all available techniques for teaching literacy, so the varying needs and capacities of individual kids can be taken into account."

- Hugh Mackay

TO
MY MOTHER

PREFATORY NOTE

The Author takes pleasure in acknowledging his indebtedness to Mr. Lorin F. Deland, of Boston, for the football play described in Chapter XV.

CONTENTS

CHAPTER I

HEROES IN MOLESKIN

"Third down, four yards to gain!"

The referee trotted out of the scrimmage line and blew his whistle; the Hillton quarter-back crouched again behind the big center; the other backs scurried to their places as though for a kick.

"*9 - 6 - 12!*" called quarter huskily.

"Get through!" shrieked the St. Eustace captain. "Block this kick!"

"*4 - 8!*"

The ball swept back to the full, the halves formed their interference, and the trio sped toward the right end of the line. For an instant the opposing ranks heaved and struggled; for an instant Hillton repelled the attack; then, like a shot, the St. Eustace left tackle hurtled through and, avoiding the interference, nailed the Hillton runner six yards back of the line. A square of the grand stand blossomed suddenly with blue, and St. Eustace's supporters, already hoarse with cheering and singing, once more broke into triumphant applause. The score-board announced fifteen minutes to play, and the ball went to the blue-clad warriors on Hillton's forty-yard line.

Hillton and St. Eustace were once more battling for supremacy on the gridiron in their annual Thanksgiving Day contest. And, in spite of the fact that Hillton was on her own grounds, St. Eustace's star was in the ascendant, and defeat hovered dark and ominous over the Crimson. With the score 5 to in favor of the visitors, with her players battered and wearied, with the second half of the game already half over, Hillton, outweighted and outplayed, fought on with the doggedness born of despair in an almost hopeless struggle to avert impending defeat.

In the first few minutes of the first half St. Eustace had battered her way down the field, throwing her heavy backs through the crimson line again and again, until she had placed the pigskin on Hillton's three-yard line. There the Hillton players had held stubbornly against two attempts to advance, but on the third down had fallen victims to a delayed pass, and St. Eustace had scored her only touch-down. The punt-out had failed, however, and the cheering flaunters of blue banners had perforce to be content with five points.

Then it was that Hillton had surprised her opponents, for when the Blue's warriors had again sought to hammer and beat their way through the opposing line they found that Hillton had awakened from her daze, and their gains were small and infrequent. Four times ere the half was at an end St. Eustace was forced to kick, and thrice, having by the hardest work and almost inch by inch fought her way to within scoring distance of her opponent's goal, she met a defense that was impregnable to her most desperate assaults. Then it was that the Crimson had waved madly over the heads of Hillton's shrieking supporters and hope had again returned to their hearts.

In the second half Hillton had secured the ball on the kick-off, and, never losing possession of it, had struggled foot by foot to within fifteen yards of the Blue's goal. From there a kick from placement had been tried, but Gale, Hillton's captain and right half-back, had been thrown before his foot had touched the leather, and the St. Eustace right-guard had fallen on the ball. A few minutes later a fumble returned the pigskin to Hillton on the Blue's thirty-three yards, and once more the advance was taken up. Thrice the distance had been gained by plunges into the line and short runs about the ends, and once Fletcher, Hillton's left half, had got away safely for twenty yards. But on her eight-yard line, under the shadow of her goal, St. Eustace had held bravely, and, securing the ball on downs, punted it far down the field into her opponent's territory. Fletcher had run it back ten yards ere he was downed, and from there it had gone six yards further by one superb hurdle by the full-back. But St. Eustace had then held finely, and on the third down, as has been told, Hillton's fake-kick play had been demolished by the Blue's tackle, and the ball was once more in the hands of St. Eustace's big center rush.

On the side-line, his hands in his pockets and his short brier pipe clenched firmly between his teeth, Gardiner, Hillton's head coach, watched grimly the tide of battle. Things had gone worse than he had anticipated. He had not hoped for too much - a tie would have satisfied him; a victory for Hillton had been beyond his expectations. St. Eustace far outweighed his team; her center was almost invulnerable and her back field was fast and heavy. But, despite the modesty of his expectations, Gardiner was disappointed. The plays that he had believed would prove to be ground-gainers had failed almost invariably. Neil Fletcher, the left half, on whom the head coach had placed the greatest reliance, had, with a single exception, failed to circle the ends for any distance. To be sure, the St. Eustace end rushes had proved more knowing than he had given them credit for being, and so the fault was, after all, not with Fletcher; but it was disappointing nevertheless.

And, as is invariably the case, he saw where he had made mistakes in the handling of his team; realized, now that it was too late, that he had given too much attention to that thing, too little to this; that, as things had turned out, certain plays discarded a week before would have proved of more value than those substituted. He sighed, and moved down the line to keep abreast of the teams, now five yards nearer the Hillton goal.

"Crozier must come out in a moment," said a voice beside him. He turned to find Professor Beck, the trainer and physical director. "What a game he has put up, eh?"

Gardiner nodded.

"Best quarter in years," he answered. "It'll weaken us considerably, but I suppose it's necessary." There was a note of interrogation in the last, and the professor heard it.

"Yes, yes, quite," he replied. "The boy's on his last legs." Gardiner turned to the line of substitutes behind them.

"Decker!"

The call was taken up by those nearest at hand, and the next instant a short, stockily-built youth was peeling off his crimson sweater. The referee's whistle blew, and while the mound of squirming players found their feet again, Gardiner walked toward them, his hand on Decker's shoulder.

"Play slow and steady your team, Decker," he counseled. "Use Young and Fletcher for runs; try them outside of tackle, especially on the right. Give Gale a chance to hit the line now and then and diversify your plays well. And, my boy, if you get that ball again, and of course you will, *don't let it go*! Give up your twenty yards if necessary, only hang on to the leather!"

Then he thumped him encouragingly on the back and sped him forward. Crozier, the deposed quarter-back, was being led off by Professor Beck. The boy was pale of face and trembling with weariness, and one foot dragged itself after the other limply. But he was protesting with tears in his eyes against being laid off, and even the hearty cheers for him that thundered from the stand did not comfort him. Then the game went on, the tide of battle flowing slowly, steadily, toward the Crimson's goal.

"If only they don't score again!" said Gardiner.

Ralph Henry Barbour

"That's the best we can hope for," said Professor Beck.

"Yes; it's turned out worse than I expected."

"Well, you can comfort yourself with the knowledge that they've played as plucky a game against odds as I ever expect to see," answered the other. "And we won't say die yet; there's still" - he looked at his watch - there's still eight minutes."

"That's good; I hope Decker will remember what I told him about runs outside right tackle," muttered Gardiner anxiously. Then he relighted his pipe and, with stolid face, watched events.

St. Eustace was still hammering Hillton's line at the wings. Time and again the Blue's big full-back plunged through between guard and tackle, now on this side, now on that, and Hillton's line ever gave back and back, slowly, stubbornly, but surely.

"First down," cried the referee. "Five yards to gain."

The pigskin now lay just midway between Hillton's ten-and fifteen-yard lines. Decker, the substitute quarter-back, danced about under the goal-posts.

"Now get through and break it up, fellows!" he shouted. "Get through! Get through!"

But the crimson-clad line men were powerless to withstand the terrific plunges of the foe, and back once more they went, and yet again, and the ball was on the six-yard line, placed there by two plunges at right tackle.

"First down!" cried the referee again.

Then Hillton's cup of sorrow seemed overflowing. For on the next play the umpire's whistle shrilled, and half the distance to the goal-line was paced off. Hillton was penalized for holding, and the ball was on her three yards!

From the section of the grand stand where the crimson flags waved came steady, entreating, the wailing slogan:

"*Hold, Hillton! Hold, Hillton! Hold, Hillton!*"

Near at hand, on the side-line, Gardiner ground his teeth on the stem of his pipe and watched with expressionless face. Professor Beck, at his side, frowned anxiously.

"Put it over, now!" cried the St. Eustace captain. "Tear them up, fellows!"

The quarter gave the signal, the two lines smashed together, and the whistle sounded. The ball had advanced less than a yard. The Hillton stand cheered hoarsely, madly.

"Line up! Line up!" cried the Blue's quarter. "Signal!"

Then it was that St. Eustace made her fatal mistake. With the memory of the delayed pass which had won St. Eustace her previous touch-down in mind, the Hillton quarter-back was on the watch.

The ball went back, was lost to view, the lines heaved and strained. Decker shot to the left, and as he reached the end of the line the St. Eustace left half-back came plunging out of the throng, the ball snuggled against his stomach. Decker, just how he never knew, squirmed past the single interferer, and tackled the runner firmly about the hips. The two went down together on the seven yards, the blue-stockinged youth vainly striving to squirm nearer to the line, Decker holding for all he was worth. Then the Hillton left end sat down suddenly on the runner's head and the whistle blew.

The grand stand was in an uproar, and cheers for Hillton filled the air. Gardiner turned away calmly and knocked the ashes from his pipe. Professor Beck beamed through his

Ralph Henry Barbour

gold-rimmed glasses. Decker picked himself up and sped back to his position.

"*Signal!*" he cried. But a St. Eustace player called for time and the whistle piped again.

"If Decker tries a kick from there it'll be blocked, and they'll score again," said Gardiner. "Our line can't hold. There's just one thing to do, but I fear Decker won't think of it." He caught Gale's eye and signaled the captain to the side-line.

"What is it?" panted that youth, taking the nose-guard from his mouth and tenderly nursing a swollen lip. Gardiner hesitated. Then -

"Nothing. Only fight it out, Gale. You've got your chance now!" Gale nodded and trotted back. Gardiner smiled ruefully. "The rule against coaching from the side-lines may be a good one," he muttered, "but I guess it's lost this game for us."

The whistle sounded and the lines formed again.

"First down," cried the referee, jumping nimbly out of the way. Decker had been in conference with the full-back, and now he sprang back to his place.

"Signal!" he cried. "*14 - 7 - 31!*"

The Hillton full stood just inside the goal-line and stretched his hands out.

"*16 - 8!*"

The center passed the pigskin straight and true to the full-back, but the latter, instead of kicking it, stood as though bewildered while the St. Eustace forwards plunged through the Hillton line as though it had been of paper. The next moment he was thrown behind his goal-line with the ball safe in his arms, and Gardiner, on the side-line, was smiling contentedly.

"Touch-back," cried Decker. "Line up on the twenty yards, fellows!"

Hillton's ruse had won her a free kick, and in another moment the ball was arching toward the St. Eustace goal. The Blue's left half secured it, but was downed on his forty yards. The first attack netted four yards through Hillton's left-guard, and the crimson flags drooped on their staffs. On the next play St. Eustace's full-back hurdled the line for two yards, but lost the pigskin, and amid frantic cries of "Ball! Ball!" Fletcher, Hillton's left half, dropped upon it. The crimson banners waved again, and Hillton voices once more took up the refrain of Hilltonians, while hope surged back into loyal hearts.

"Five minutes to play," said Professor Beck. Gardiner nodded.

"Time enough to win in," he answered.

Decker crouched again, chanted his signal, and the Hillton full plunged at the blue-clad line. But only a yard resulted.

"*Signal*!" cried the quarter. "*8 - 51 - 16 - 5*!"

The ball came back into his waiting hands, was thrown at a short pass to the left half, and, with right half showing the way and full-back charging along beside, Fletcher cleared the line through a wide gap outside of St. Eustace's right tackle and sped down the field while the Hillton supporters leaped to their feet and shrieked wildly. The full-back met the St. Eustace right half, and the two were left behind on the turf. Beside Fletcher, a little in advance, ran the Hillton captain and right half-back, Paul Gale. Between them and the goal, now forty yards away, only the St. Eustace quarter remained, but behind them came pounding footsteps that sounded dangerous.

Gardiner, followed by the professor and a little army of privileged spectators, raced along the line.

Ralph Henry Barbour

"He'll make it," muttered the head coach. "They can't stop him!"

One line after another went under the feet of the two players. The pursuit was falling behind. Twenty yards remained to be covered. Then the waiting quarter-back, white-faced and desperate, was upon them. But Gale was equal to the emergency.

"To the left!" he panted.

Fletcher obeyed with weary limbs and leaden feet, and without looking knew that he was safe. Gale and the St. Eustace player went down together, and in another moment Fletcher was lying, faint but happy, over the line and back of the goal!

The stands emptied themselves on the instant of their triumphant burden of shouting, cheering, singing Hilltonians, and the crimson banners waved and fluttered on to the field. Hillton had escaped defeat!

But Fortune, now that she had turned her face toward the wearers of the Crimson, had further gifts to bestow. And presently, when the wearied and crestfallen opponents had lined themselves along the goal-line, Decker held the ball amid a breathless silence, and Hillton's right end sent it fair and true between the uprights: Hillton, 6; Opponents, 5.

The game, so far as scoring went, ended there. Four minutes later the whistle shrilled for the last time, and the horde of frantic Hilltonians flooded the field and, led by the band, bore their heroes in triumph back to the school. And, side by side, at the head of the procession, perched on the shoulders of cheering friends, swayed the two half-backs, Neil Fletcher and Paul Gale.

CHAPTER II

PAUL CHANGES HIS MIND

Two boys were sitting in the first-floor corner study in Haewood's. Those who know the town of Hillton, New York, will remember Haewood's as the large residence at the corner of Center and Village Streets, from the big bow-window of which the occupant of the cushioned seat may look to the four points of the compass or watch for occasional signs of life about the court-house diagonally across. To-night - the bell in the tower of the town hall had just struck half after seven - the occupants of the corner study were interested in things other than the view.

I have said that they were sitting. Lounging would be nearer the truth; for one, a boy of eighteen years, with merry blue eyes and cheeks flushed ruddily with health and the afterglow of the day's excitement, with hair just the color of raw silk that took on a glint of gold where the light fell upon it, was perched cross-legged amid the cushions at one end of the big couch, two strong, tanned, and much-scarred hands clasping his knees. His companion and his junior by but two months, a dark-complexioned youth with black hair and eyes and a careless, good-natured, but rather wilful face, on which at the present moment the most noticeable feature was a badly cut and much swollen lower lip, lay sprawled at the other end of the couch, his chin buried in one palm.

Both lads were well built, broad of chest, and long of limb,

Ralph Henry Barbour

with bright, clear eyes, and a warmth of color that betokened the best of physical condition. They had been friends and room-mates for two years. This was their last year at Hillton, and next fall they were to begin their college life together. The dark-complexioned youth rolled lazily on to his back and stared at the ceiling. Then -

"I suppose Crozier will get the captaincy, Neil."

The boy with light hair nodded without removing his gaze from the little flames that danced in the fireplace. They had discussed the day's happenings thoroughly, had relived the game with St. Eustace from start to finish, and now the big Thanksgiving dinner which they had eaten was beginning to work upon them a spell of dormancy. It was awfully jolly, thought Neil Fletcher, to just lie there and watch the flames and - and - He sighed comfortably and closed his eyes. At eight o'clock he, with the rest of the victorious team, was to be drawn about the town in a barge and cheered at, but meanwhile there was time to just close his eyes - and forget - everything -

There was a knock at the study door.

"Go 'way!" grunted Neil.

"Oh, come in," called Paul Gale, without, however, removing his drowsy gaze from the ceiling or changing his position.

"I beg your pardon. I am looking for Mr. Gale, and -"

Paul dropped his legs over the side of the couch and sat up, blinking at the visitor. Neil followed his example. The caller was a carefully dressed man of about thirty-five, scarcely taller than Neil, but broader of shoulder. Paul recognized him, and, rising, shook hands.

"How do you do, Mr. Brill? Glad to see you. Sit down, won't you? I guess we were both pretty nigh asleep when you knocked."

"Small wonder," responded the visitor affably. "After the work you did this afternoon you deserve sleep, and anything else you want." He laid aside his coat and hat and sank into the chair which Paul proffered.

"By the way," continued the latter, "I don't think you've met my friend, Neil Fletcher. Neil, this is Mr. Brill, of Robinson; one of their coaches." The two shook hands.

"I'm delighted to meet the hero - I should say one of the heroes - of the day," said Mr. Brill. "That run was splendid; the way in which you two fellows got your speed up before you reached the line was worth coming over here to see, really it was."

"Yes, Paul set a pretty good pace," answered Neil.

The visitor discussed the day's contest for a few minutes, during which Neil glanced uneasily from time to time at the clock, wondered what the visitor wanted there, and heartily wished he'd take himself off. But presently Mr. Brill got down to business.

"You know we've had a little victory in football ourselves this fall," he was saying. "We won from Erskine by 17 to 6 last week, and we're feeling rather stuck up over it."

"Wait till next year," said Neil to himself, "and you'll get over it."

"And that," continued the coach, "brings me to the object of my call tonight. Frankly, we want you two fellows at Robinson College, and I'm here to see if we can't have you." He paused and smiled engagingly at the boys. Neil glanced surprisedly at Paul, who was thoughtfully examining the scars on his knuckles. "Don't decide until I've explained matters more clearly," went on the visitor. "Perhaps neither of you have been to Collegetown, but at least you know about where Robinson stands in the athletic world, and you know that as an institution of learning it is in the front rank of the smaller colleges; in fact, in certain lines it might dispute the place of honor with some of the big ones.

"To the fellow who wants a college where he can learn and where, at the same time, he can give some attention to athletics, Robinson's bound to recommend itself. I mention this because you know as well as I do that there are colleges - I mention no names - where a born football player, such as either of you, would simply be lost; where he would be tied down by such stringent rules that he could never amount to anything on the gridiron. I don't mean to say that at Robinson the faculty is lax regarding standing or attendance at lectures, but I do say that it holds common-sense views on the subject of college athletics, and does not hound a man to death simply because he happens to belong to the football eleven or the crew.

"Robinson is always on the lookout for first-class football, baseball, or rowing material, and she believes in offering encouragement to such material. She doesn't favor underhand methods, you understand; no hiring of players, no free scholarships - though there are plenty of them for those who will work for them - none of that sort of thing. But she is willing to meet you half-way. The proposition which I am authorized to make is briefly this" - the speaker leaned forward, smiling frankly, and tapped a forefinger on the palm of his other hand - "If you, Mr. Gale, and you, Mr. Fletcher, will enter Robinson next September, the - ah - the athletic authorities will guarantee you positions on the varsity eleven. Besides this, you will be given free tutoring for the entrance exams, and afterward, so long as you remain on the team, in any studies with which you may have difficulty. Now, there is a fair, honest proposition, and one which I sincerely trust you will accept. We want you both, and we're willing to do all that we can - in honesty, that is - to get you. Now, what do you say?"

During this recital Neil's dislike of the speaker had steadily increased, and now, under the other's smiling regard, he had difficulty in keeping from his face some show of his emotions. Paul looked up from his scarred knuckles and eyed Neil furtively before he turned to the coach.

"Of course," he said, "this is rather unexpected."

The coach's eyes flickered for an instant with amusement.

"For my part," Neil broke in almost angrily, "I'm due in September at Erskine, and unless Paul's changed his mind since yesterday so's he."

The Robinson coach raised his eyebrows in simulated surprise.

"Ah," he said slowly, "Erskine?"

"Yes, Erskine," answered Neil rather discourteously. A faint flush of displeasure crept into Mr. Brill's cheeks, but he smiled as pleasantly as ever.

"And your friend has contemplated ruining his football career in the same manner, has he?" he asked politely, turning his gaze as he spoke on Paul. The latter fidgeted in his chair and looked over a trifle defiantly at his room-mate.

"I had thought of going to Erskine," he answered. "In fact" - observing Neil's wide-eyed surprise at his choice of words - "in fact, I had arranged to do so. But - but, of course, nothing has been settled definitely."

"But, Paul -" exclaimed Neil.

"Well, I'm glad to hear that," interrupted Mr. Brill. "For in my opinion it would simply be a waste of your opportunities and - ah - abilities, Mr. Gale."

"Well, of course, if a fellow doesn't have to bother too much about studies," said Paul haltingly, "he can do better work on the team; there can't be any question about that, I guess."

"None at all," responded the coach.

Neil stared at his chum indignantly.

"You're talking rot," he growled. Paul flushed and returned his look angrily.

"I suppose I have the right to manage my own affairs?" he demanded. Neil realized his mistake and, with an effort, held his peace. Mr. Brill turned to him.

"I fear there's no use in attempting to persuade you to come to us also?" he said. Neil shook his head silently. Then, realizing that Paul was quite capable, in his present fit of stubbornness, of promising to enter Robinson if only to spite his room-mate, Neil used guile.

"Anyhow, September's a long way off," he said, "and I don't see that it's necessary to decide to-night. Perhaps we had both better take a day or two to think it over. I guess Mr. Brill won't insist on a final answer to-night."

The Robinson coach hesitated, but then answered readily enough:

"Certainly not. Think it over; only, if possible, let me hear your decision to-morrow, as I am leaving town then."

"Well, as far as I'm concerned," said Paul, "I don't see any use in putting it off. I'm willing -"

Neil jumped to his feet. A burst of martial music swept up to them as the school band, followed by a host of their fellows, turned the corner of the building.

"Come on, Paul," he cried; "get your coat on. Mr. Brill will excuse us if we leave him; we mustn't keep the fellows waiting. And we can think the matter over, eh, Paul? And we'll let him know in the morning. Here's your coat. Good-night, sir, good-night." He was holding the door open and smiling politely. Paul, scowling, arose and shook hands with the Robinson emissary. Neil kept up a steady stream of talk, and his chum could only mutter vague words about his pleasure at Mr. Brill's call and about seeing him to-morrow. When the door had closed behind him the coach stood a moment in the hall and thoughtfully buttoned his coat.

"I think I've got Gale all right," he said to himself, "but" - with a slight smile - "the other chap was too smart for me. And, confound him, he's just the sort we need!"

When he reached the entrance he was obliged to elbow his way through a solid throng of shouting youths who with excited faces and waving caps and flags informed the starlight winter sky over and over that they wanted Gale and Fletcher, to which demand the band lent hearty if rather discordant emphasis.

*   *   *   *   *

A good deal happened in the next two hours, but nothing that is pertinent to this narrative. Victorious Hillton elevens have been hauled through the village and out to the field many times in past years, and bonfires have flared and speeches have been made by players and faculty, and all very much as happened on this occasion. Neil and Paul returned to their room at ten o'clock, tired, happy, with the cheers and the songs still echoing in their ears.

Paul had apparently forgotten his resentment toward Neil and the whole matter of Brill's proposition. But Neil hadn't, and presently, when they were preparing for bed, he returned doggedly to the charge.

"When did you meet that fellow Brill?" he asked.

"In Gardiner's room this morning; he introduced us." Paul began to look sulky again. "Seems a decent sort, I think," he added defiantly. Neil accepted the challenge.

"I dare say," he answered carelessly. "There's only one thing I've got against him."

"What's that?" questioned Paul suspiciously.

"His errand."

"What's wrong with his errand?"

"Everything, Paul. You know as well as I that his offer is - well, it's shady, to say the least. Who ever heard of a decent college offering free tutoring in order to get fellows for its football team?"

"Lots of them do," growled Paul.

"No, they don't; not decent ones. Some do, I know; but they're not colleges a fellow cares to go to. Every one knows what rotten shape Robinson athletics are in; the papers have been full of it for two years. Their center rush this fall, Harden, just went there to play on the team, and everybody says that he got his tuition free. You don't want to play on a team like that and have people say things like that about you. I'm sure I don't."

"Oh, you!" sneered Paul. "You're getting crankier and crankier every day. I'll bet you're just huffy because Brill didn't ask you first."

Neil flushed, but kept his temper.

"You don't think anything of the sort, Paul. Besides -"

"It looks that way," muttered Paul.

"Besides," continued Neil calmly, "what's the advantage in going to Robinson? We've arranged everything; we've got our rooms picked out at Erskine; there are lots of fellows there we know; the college is the best of its class and its athletics are honest. If you play on the Erskine team you'll be somebody, and folks won't hint that you're receiving money or free scholarships or something for doing it. And as for Brill's guarantee of a place on the team, why, there's only one decent way to get on a football team, and that's by good, hard work; and there's no reason for doubting that you'll make the Erskine varsity eleven."

"Yes, there is, too," answered Paul angrily. "They've got lots of good players at Erskine, and you and I won't stand any better show than a dozen others."

"I don't want to."

"Huh! Well, I do; that is, I want to make the team. Besides, as Brill said, if a fellow has the faculty after him all the time about studies he can't do decent work on the team. I don't see anything wrong in it, and - and I'm going. I'll tell Brill so to-morrow!"

Neil drew his bath-robe about him, and looked thoughtfully into the flames. So far he had lost, but he had one more card to play. He turned and faced Paul's angry countenance.

"Well, if I should go to Robinson and play on her team under the conditions offered by that - by Brill I'd feel disgraced."

"You'd better stay away, then," answered Paul hotly.

"I wouldn't want to show my face around Hillton afterward, and if I met Gardiner or 'Wheels' I'd take the other side of the street."

"Oh, you would?" cried his room-mate. "You're trying to make yourself out a little fluffy angel, aren't you? And I suppose I'm not good enough to associate with you, am I? Well, if that's it, all I've got to say -"

"But," continued Neil equably, "if you accept Brill's offer, so will I."

Paul paused open-mouthed and stared at his chum. Then his eyes dropped and he busied himself with a stubborn stocking. Finally, with a muttered "Humph!" he gathered up his clothing and disappeared into the bedroom. Neil turned and smiled at the flames and, finding his own apparel, followed. Nothing more was said. Paul splashed the water about even more than usual and tumbled silently into bed. Neil put out the study light and followed suit.

"Good-night," he said.

"Good-night," growled Paul.

It had been a hard day and an exciting one, and Neil went to sleep almost as soon as his head touched the pillow. It seemed hours later, though in reality but some twenty minutes, that he was awakened by hearing his name called. He sat up quickly.

"Hello! What?" he shouted.

"Shut up," answered Paul from across in the darkness. "I didn't know you were asleep. I only wanted to say - to tell you - that - that I've decided not to go to Robinson!"

CHAPTER III

IN NEW QUARTERS

Almost every one has heard of Erskine College. For the benefit of the few who have not, and lest they confound it with Williams or Dartmouth or Bowdoin or some other of its New England neighbors, it may be well to tell something about it. Erskine College is still in its infancy, as New England universities go, with its centennial yet eight years distant. But it has its own share of historic associations, and although the big elm in the center of the campus was not planted until 1812 it has shaded many youths who in later years have by good deeds and great accomplishments endeared themselves to country and alma mater.

In the middle of the last century, when Erskine was little more than an academy, it was often called "the little green school at Centerport." It is not so little now, but it's greener than ever. Wide-spreading elms grow everywhere; in serried ranks within the college grounds, in smaller detachments throughout the village, in picket lines along the river and out into the country. The grass grows lush wherever it can gain hold, and, not content with having its own way on green and campus, is forever attempting the conquest of path and road. The warm red bricks of the college buildings are well-nigh hidden by ivy, which, too, is an ardent expansionist. And where neither grass nor ivy can subjugate, soft, velvety moss reigns humbly.

In the year 1901, which is the period of this story, the

enrolment in all departments at Erskine was close to six hundred students. The freshman class, as had been the case for many years past, was the largest in the history of the college. It numbered 180; but of this number we are at present chiefly interested in only two; and these two, at the moment when this chapter begins - which, to be exact, is eight o'clock of the evening of the twenty-fourth day of September in the year above mentioned - were busily at work in a first-floor study in the boarding-house of Mrs. Curtis on Elm Street.

It were perhaps more truthful to say that one was busily at work and the other was busily advising and directing. Neil Fletcher stood on a small table, which swayed perilously from side to side at his every movement, and drove nails into an already much mutilated wall. Paul Gale sat in a hospitable armchair upholstered in a good imitation of green leather and nodded approval.

"That'll do for 'Old Abe'; now hang The First Snow a bit to the left and underneath."

"The First Snow hasn't any wire on it," complained Neil. "See if you can't find some."

"Wire's all gone," answered Paul. "We'll have to get some more. Where's that list? Oh, here it is. 'Item, picture wire.' I say, what in thunder's this you've got down - 'Ring for waistband'?"

"Rug for wash-stand, you idiot! I guess we'll have to quit until we get some more wire, eh? Or we might hang a few of them with boot-laces and neckties?"

"Oh, let's call it off. I'm tired," answered Paul with a grin. "The room begins to look rather decent, doesn't it? We must change that couch, though; put it the other way so the ravelings won't show. And that picture of -"

But just here Neil attempted to step from the table and landed in a heap on the floor, and Paul forgot criticism in joyful applause.

"Oh, noble work! Do it again, old man; I didn't see the take-off!"

But Neil refused, and plumping himself into a wicker rocking-chair that creaked complainingly, rubbed the dust from his hands to his trousers and looked about the study approvingly.

"We're going to be jolly comfy here, Paul," he said. "Mrs. Curtis is going to get a new globe for that fixture over there."

"Then we will be," said Paul. "And if she would only find us a towel-rack that didn't fall into twelve separate pieces like a Chinese puzzle every time a chap put a towel on it we'd be simply reveling in luxury."

"I think I can fix that thing with string," answered Neil. "Or we might buy one of those nickel-plated affairs that you screw into the wall."

"The sort that always dump the towels on to the floor, you mean? Yes, we might. Of course, they're of no practical value judged as towel-racks, but they're terribly ornamental. You know we had one in the bath-room at the beach. Remember? When you got through your bath and groped round for the towel it was always lying on the floor just out of reach."

"Yes, I remember," answered Neil, smiling. "We had rather a good time, didn't we, at Seabright? It was awfully nice of you to ask me down there, Paul; and your folks were mighty good to me. Next summer I want you to come up to New Hampshire and see us for a while. Of course, we can't give you sea bathing, and you won't look like a red Indian when you go home, but we could have a good time just the same."

"Red Indian yourself!" cried Paul. "You're nearly twice as tanned as I am. I don't see how you did it. I was there pretty near all summer and you stayed just three weeks; and look at us! I'm as white as a sheet of paper -"

"Yes, brown paper," interpolated Neil.

"And you have a complexion like a - a football after a hard game."

Neil grinned, then -

"By the way," he said, "did I tell you I'd heard from Crozier?"

"About Billy and the ducks? And Gordon's not going back to Hillton? Yes, you got that at the beach; remember?"

"So I did. 'Old Cro' will be up to his ears in trouble pretty soon, won't he? I'm glad they made him captain, awfully glad. I think he can turn out a team that'll rub it into St. Eustace again just as you did last year."

"Yes; and Gardiner's going to coach again." Paul smiled reminiscently. Then, "By Jove, it does seem funny not to be going back to old Hillton, doesn't it? I suppose after a while a fellow'll get to feeling at home here, but just at present -" He sighed and shook his head.

"Wait until college opens to-morrow and we get to work; we won't have much time to feel much of anything, I guess. Practise is called for four o'clock. I wonder - I wonder if we'll make the team?"

"Why not?" objected Paul. "If I thought I wouldn't I think I'd pitch it all up and - and go to Robinson!" He grinned across at his chum.

"You stay here and you'll get a chance to go *at* Robinson; that's a heap more satisfactory."

"Well, I'm going to make the varsity, Neil. I've set my heart on that, and what I make up my mind to do I sometimes most always generally do. I'm not troubling, my boy; I'll show them a few tricks about playing half-back that'll open their eyes. You wait and see!"

Neil looked as though he was not quite certain as to that, but said nothing, and Paul went on:

"I wonder what sort of a fellow this Devoe is?"

"Well, I've never seen him, but we know that he's about as good an end as there is in college to-day; and I guess he's bound to be the right sort or they wouldn't have made him captain."

"He's a senior, isn't he?"

"Yes; he's played only two years, and they say he's going into the Yale Law School next year. If he does, of course he'll get on the team there. Well, I hope he'll take pity on two ambitious but unprotected freshmen and -"

There was a knock at the study door and Paul jumped forward and threw it open. A tall youth of twenty-one or twenty-two years of age stood in the doorway.

"I'm looking for Mr. Gale and Mr. Fletcher. Have I hit it right?"

"I'm Gale," answered Paul, "and that's Fletcher. Won't you come in?" The visitor entered.

"My name's Devoe," he explained smilingly. "I'm captain of the football team this year, and as you two fellows are, of course, going to try for the team, I thought we'd better get acquainted." He accepted the squeaky rocking-chair and allowed Paul to take his straw hat. Neil thought he'd ought to shake hands, but as Devoe made no move in that direction he retired to another seat and grinned hospitably instead.

"I've heard of the good work you chaps did for Hillton last year, and I was mighty glad when I learned from Gardiner that you were coming up here."

"You know Gardiner?" asked Neil.

"No, I've never met him, but of course every football man knows who he is. He wrote to me in the spring that you were coming, and rather intimated that if I knew my business I'd keep an eye on you and see that you didn't get lost in the shuffle. So here I am."

"He didn't say anything about having written," pondered Neil.

"Oh, he wouldn't," answered Devoe. "Well, how do you like us as far as you've seen us?"

"We only got here yesterday," replied Paul. "I think it looks like rather a jolly sort of place; awfully pretty, you know, and - er - historic."

"Yes, it is pretty; historic too; and it's the finest young college in the country, bar none," answered Devoe. "You'll like it when you get used to it. I like it so well I wish I wasn't going to leave it in the spring. Very cozy quarters you have here." He looked about the study.

"They'll do," answered Neil modestly. "Of course we couldn't get rooms in the Yard, and we liked this as well as anything we saw outside. The view's rather good from the windows."

"Yes, I know; you have the common and pretty much the whole college in sight; it is good." Devoe brought his gaze back and fixed it on Neil. "You played left half, didn't you?"

"Yes."

"What's your weight?"

"I haven't weighed this summer," answered Neil. "In the spring I was a hundred and sixty-two."

"Good. We need some heavy backs. How about you, Gale?"

"About a hundred and sixty."

"Of course I haven't seen the new material yet," continued Devoe, "but the last year's men we have are a bit light, take them all around. That's what beat us, you see; Robinson had an unusually heavy line and rather heavy backs. They plowed through us without trouble."

Neil studied the football captain with some interest. He saw a tall and fairly heavy youth, with well-set head and broad shoulders. He looked quite as fast on his feet as rumor credited him with being, and his dark eyes, sharp and steady in their regard, suggested both courage and ability to lead. His other features were strong, the nose a trifle heavy, the mouth usually unsmiling, the chin determined, and the forehead, set off by carefully brushed dark-brown hair, high and broad. After the first few moments of conversation Devoe devoted his attention principally to Neil, questioning him regarding Gardiner's coaching methods, about Neil's experience on the gridiron, as to what studies he was taking up. Occasionally he included Paul in the conversation, but that youth discovered, with surprise and chagrin, that he was apparently of much less interest to Devoe than was Neil. After a while he dropped out of the talk altogether, save when directly appealed to, and sat silent with an expression of elaborate unconcern. At the end of half an hour Devoe arose.

"I must be getting on," he announced. "I'm glad we've had this talk, and I hope you'll both come over some evening and call on me; I'm in Morris, No. 8. We've got our work cut out this fall, and I hope we'll all pull together." He smiled across at Paul, evidently unaware of having neglected that young gentleman in his conversation. "Good-night. Four o'clock to-morrow is the hour."

Ralph Henry Barbour

"I never met any one that could ask more questions than he can," exclaimed Neil when Devoe was safely out of hearing. "But I suppose that's the way to learn, eh?"

Paul yawned loudly and shrugged his shoulders.

"Funny he should have come just when we were talking about him, wasn't it?" Neil pursued. "What do you think of him?"

"Well, if you ask me," Paul answered, "I think he's a conceited, stuck-up prig!"

CHAPTER IV

NEIL MAKES ACQUAINTANCES

Neil's and Paul's college life began early the next morning when, sitting side by side in the dim, hushed chapel, they heard white-haired Dr. Garrison ask for them divine aid and guidance. Splashes and flecks of purple and rose and golden light rested here and there on bowed head and shoulders or lay in shafts across the aisles. From where he sat Neil could look through an open window out into the morning world of greenery and sunlight. On the swaying branch of an elm that almost brushed the casement a thrush sang sweet and clear a matin of his own. Neil made several good resolutions that morning there in the chapel, some of which he profited by, all of which he sincerely meant. And even Paul, far less impressionable than his friend, looked uncommonly thoughtful all the way back to their room, a way that led through the elm-arched nave of College Place and across the common with its broad expanses of sun-flecked sward and its simple granite shaft commemorating the heroes of the civil war.

At nine o'clock, with the sound of the pealing bell again in their ears, with their books under their arms and their hearts beating a little faster than usual with pleasurable excitement, they retraced their path and mounted the well-worn granite steps of College Hall for their first recitation. What with the novelty of it all the day passed quickly enough, and four o'clock found the two lads dressed in football togs and awaiting the beginning of practise.

Ralph Henry Barbour

There were some sixty candidates in sight, boys - some of them men as far as years go - of all sizes and ages, several at the first glance revealing the hopelessness of their ambitions. The names were taken and fall practise at Erskine began.

The candidates were placed on opposite sides of the gridiron, and half a dozen footballs were produced. Punting and catching punts was the order of the day, and Neil was soon busily at work. The afternoon was warm, but not uncomfortably so, the turf was springy underfoot, the sky was blue from edge to edge, the new men supplied plenty of amusement in their efforts, the pigskins bumped into his arms in the manner of old friends, and Neil was happy as a lark. After one catch for which he had to run back several yards, he let himself out and booted the leather with every ounce of strength. The ball sailed high in a long arching flight, and sent several men across the field scampering back into the grand stand for it.

"I guess you've done that before," said a voice beside him. A short, stockily-built youth with a round, smiling face and blue eyes that twinkled with fun and good spirits was observing him shrewdly.

"Yes," answered Neil, "I have."

"I thought so," was the reply. "But you're a freshman, aren't you?"

"Yes," answered Neil, turning to let a low drive from across the gridiron settle into his arms. "And I guess you're not."

"No, this is my third year. I've been on the team two." He paused to send a ball back, and then wiped the perspiration from his forehead. "I was quarter last year."

"Oh," said Neil, observing his neighbor with interest, "then you're Foster?"

"That's me. What are you trying for?"

"Half-back. I played three years at Hillton."

"Of course; you're the fellow Bob Devoe was talking about - or one of them; I think he said there were two of you. Which one are you?"

"I'm the other one," laughed Neil. "I'm Fletcher. That's Gale over there, the fellow in the old red shirt; he was our captain at Hillton last year."

Foster looked across at Paul and then back at Neil. He was evidently comparing them. He shook his head.

"It's a good thing he's got dark hair and you've got light," he said. "Otherwise you wouldn't know yourselves apart; you're just of a height and build, and weight, too, I guess. Are you related?"

"No. But we are pretty much the same height and weight. He's half an inch taller, and I think I weigh two pounds more."

In the intervals of catching and returning punts the acquaintance ripened. When, at the end of three-quarters of an hour, Devoe gave the order to quit and the trainer sent them twice about the gridiron on a trot, Neil found Foster ambling along beside him.

"Phew!" exclaimed the latter. "I guess I lived too high last summer and put on weight. This is taking it out of me finely; I can feel whole pounds melting off. It doesn't seem to bother you any," he added.

"No, I haven't much flesh about me," panted Neil; "but I'm glad this is the last time around, just the same!"

After their baths in the little green-roofed locker-house the two walked back to the yard together, Paul, as Neil saw, being in close companionship with a big youth whose name, according to Foster, was Tom Cowan.

"He played right-guard last year," said Foster. "He's a soph; this is his third year."

"Third year!" exclaimed Neil. "But how -"

"Oh, Cowan was too busy to pass his exams last year," said Foster with a grin. "So they let him stay a soph. He doesn't care; a little thing like that never bothers Cowan." His tone was rather contemptuous.

"Is he liked?" Neil asked.

"Oh, yes; he's very popular among a small and select circle of friends - a very small circle." Then he dismissed Cowan with an airy wave of one hand. "By the way," he continued, "have you any candidate for the presidency of your class?"

"No," Neil replied. "I haven't heard anything about it yet."

"Good; then you can vote for 'Fan' Livingston. He's a *protege* of mine, you see; used to know him at St. Mathias; you'll like him. He's an awfully good, manly, straightforward chap, just the fellow for the place. The election comes off next Thursday evening. How about your friend?"

"Gale? I don't think he has any one in view. I guess you can count on his vote, too."

"Thanks; just mention it to him, will you? I'm booming Livingston, and I want to see him win. Can't you come round some evening the first of the week? I'd like you to meet him. And meanwhile just talk him up a bit, will you?"

Neil promised and made an appointment to meet the candidate the following Saturday night at Foster's room in McLean Hall. The two parted at the gate, Foster going up to his room and Neil traversing the campus and the common to his own quarters. As he opened the study door he was surprised to hear voices within. Paul and his new acquaintance,

Tom Cowan, were sitting side by side on the window-seat.

"Hello," greeted the former. "How'd it go? Like old times, wasn't it? Neil, I want you to meet Mr. Cowan. Cowan has quarters up-stairs here. He's an old player, and we've been telling each other how good we are."

Cowan looked for an instant as though he didn't quite appreciate the latter remark, but summoned a smile as he shook hands with Neil and complimented him on his playing in Hillton's last game with St. Eustace. Neil replied with extraordinary politeness. He was always extraordinarily polite to persons he didn't fancy, and his dislike of Cowan was instant and hearty. Cowan looked to be fully twenty-three years old, and owned to being twenty-one. He was fully six feet two, and apparently weighed about two hundred pounds. His face was rather handsome in a coarse, heavy-featured style, and his hands, as Neil observed, were not quite clean. Later, Neil discovered that they never were.

After listening politely for some moments to Cowan's tales of former football triumphs and defeats, in all of which the narrator played, according to his words, a prominent part, Neil broke into the stream of his eloquence and told Paul of his meeting with Foster, and of their talk regarding the freshman presidency.

"Well," answered Paul, smiling at Cowan, "you'll have to get out of that promise to Foster or whatever his name is, because we've got a plan better than that. The fact is, Neil, I'm going to try for the presidency myself!"

"I suppose you're fooling?" gasped Neil.

"Not a bit! Why shouldn't I have a fling at it? Cowan here has promised to help; in fact, it was he that suggested it. With his help and yours, and with the kind assistance of one or two fellows I know here, I daresay I can pull out on top. Anyhow, there's no harm in trying."

"I think you'll win," said Cowan. "This chump Livingston that Foster is booming is a regular milksop; does nothing but grind, so they say; came out of St. Mathias with all kinds of silly prizes and such. What the fellows always want is a good, popular chap that goes in for athletics and that will make a name for himself."

"Foster said Livingston was something of a dab at baseball," said Neil.

"Baseball!" cried Cowan. "What's baseball? Why not puss-in-the-corner? A chap with a football reputation like Gale here can walk all round your baseball man. We'll carry it with a rush! You'll see! Freshmen are like a lot of sheep - show 'em the way and they'll fall over themselves to get there."

"Well, we're freshmen ourselves, you know," said Neil sweetly. Cowan looked nonplussed for a moment. Then -

"Oh, but you fellows are different; you've got sense. I was speaking of the general run of freshmen," he explained.

"Thanks," murmured Neil. Paul scented danger.

"I'll put the campaign in your hands and Cowan's, Neil," he said. "You know several fellows here - there's Wallace and Knowles and Jones. They're not freshmen, but they can give you introductions. Knowles is a St. Agnes man and there are lots of St. Agnes fellows in our class."

"I think you're making a mistake," answered Neil soberly, "and I wish you'd give it up. Livingston's got lots of supporters, and he's had his campaign under way for a week. If you're defeated I think it'll hurt you; fellows don't like defeated candidates when - when they're self-appointed candidates."

"Oh, of course, if you don't want to help," cried Paul, with a trace of anger in his voice, "I guess we can get on without you."

"I'm sure you won't desert your chum, Fletcher," said Cowan. "And I think you're all wrong about defeated candidates. If a fellow makes a good fight and is worsted no fellow that isn't a cad does other than honor him."

"Well, if you've made up your mind, Paul," answered Neil reluctantly, "of course I'll do all I can if Foster will let me out of my promise to him."

"Oh, hang Foster!" cried Cowan. "He's a little fool!"

"Is he?" asked Neil innocently. "I hadn't noticed it. Well, as I say, I'll do all I can. And I'll begin now by going over to see him."

"That's the boy," said Paul. "Tell Foster there's a dark horse in the field."

"And tell him I say the dark horse will win," added Cowan.

Neil smiled back politely from the doorway.

"I don't think I'd better mention your name, Mr. Cowan." He closed the door behind him, leaving Cowan much puzzled as to the meaning of the last remark, and sought No. 12 McLean. He found the varsity quarter-back writing a letter by means of a small typewriter, his brow heavily creased with scowls and his feet kicking exasperatedly at the legs of his chair.

"Hello," was Foster's greeting. "Come in. And, I say, just look around on the floor there, will you, and see if you can find an L."

"Find what?" asked Neil, searching the carpet with his gaze.

"An L. There was one on this pesky machine a while ago, but I - can't - find - Ah, here it is! 'L-O-V-I-N-G-L-Y, T-E-D'! There, that's done. I bought this idiotic thing because some one said you could write letters on it in half the time it takes with a pen. Well, I began this letter last night, and I guess I've spent fully two hours on it altogether. For two cents I'd pitch it out the window!" He pushed back his chair and glared vindictively at the typewriter. "And look at the result!" He held up a sheet of paper half covered with strange characters and erasures. "Look how I've spelled 'allowance' - alliwzee! Do you think dad will know what I mean?"

Neil shook his head dubiously.

"Not unless he's looking for the word," he answered.

"Well, he will be," grinned Foster. "Don't suppose you want to buy a fine typewriter at half price, do you?"

Neil was sure he didn't and broached the subject of his call. Foster showed some amazement when he learned of Gale's candidacy, but at once absolved Neil from his promise.

"Frankly, Fletcher, I don't think your friend has the ghost of a show, you know, but, of course, if he wants to try it it's all right. And I'm just as much obliged to you."

During the next week Neil worked early and late for Paul's success. He made some converts, but not enough to give him much hope. Livingston was easily the popular candidate for the presidency, and Neil failed to understand where Cowan found ground for the encouraging reports that he made to Paul. Paul himself was hopeful all the way through, and lent ill attention to Neil's predictions of failure.

"You always were a raven, chum," he would exclaim. "Wait until Thursday night."

And Neil, without much hope, waited.

CHAPTER V

AND SHOWS HIS METTLE

The freshman election took place in one of the lecture rooms of Grace Hall. There was a full attendance of the entering class, while the absence of sophomores was considered by those who had heard of former freshman elections at Erskine as something unnatural and of evil portent.

Paul, robbed of the support of Tom Cowan's presence, was noticeably ill at ease, and for the first time appeared to be in doubt as to his election. Fanwell Livingston was put in nomination by one of his St. Mathias friends in a speech that secured wide applause, and the nomination was duly seconded by a red-headed and very eloquent youth who, so Neil learned, was King, the captain of the St. Mathias baseball team of the preceding spring.

"Are there any more nominations?" asked the chairman, a member of the junior class.

South, a Hillton boy, arose and spoke at some length of the courage and ability for leadership of one of whom they had all heard; "of one who on the white-grilled field of battle had successfully led the hosts of Hillton Academy against the St. Eustace hosts." (Two St. Eustace graduates howled derisively.) South ended in a wild burst of flowery eloquence and placed in nomination "that triumphant football captain, that best of good fellows, Paul Dunlop Gale!"

The applause which followed was flattering, though, had Paul but known it, it was rather for the speech than the nominee. And the effect was somewhat marred by several inquiries from different parts of the hall as to who in thunder Gale was. Neil secured recognition ere the applause had subsided, and seconded the nomination. He avoided rhetoric, and told his classmates in few words and simple phrases that Paul Gale possessed pluck, generalship, and executive ability; that he had proved this at Hillton, and, given the chance, would prove it again at Erskine.

"Gale is a stranger to many of you fellows," he concluded, "but, whether you make him class president or whether you give that honor to another, he won't be a stranger long. A fellow that can pilot a Hillton football team to victory against almost overwhelming odds and through the greatest of difficulties as Gale did last year is not the sort to sit around in corners and watch the procession go by. No, sir; keep your eye on him. I'll wager that before the year's out you'll be prouder of him than of any man in your class. And, meanwhile, if you're looking for the right man for the presidency, a man that'll lead 1905 to a renown beside which the other classes will look like so many battered golf-balls, why, I've told you where to look."

Neil sat down amid a veritable roar of applause, and Paul, totally unembarrassed by the praise and acclaim, smiled with satisfaction. "That was all right, chum," he whispered. "I guess we've got them on the run, eh?"

But Neil shook his head doubtfully. Cries of "Vote! Vote!" arose, and in a moment or two the balloting began. While this was proceeding announcement was made that the annual Freshman Class Dinner would be held on the evening of the following Monday, October 7th. When the cheers occasioned by this information had subsided the chairman arose.

"The result of the balloting, gentlemen," he announced, "is as follows: Livingston, 97; Gale, 45. Mr. Livingston is elected by a majority of 52."

Shouts of "Livingston! Livingston! Speech! Speech!" filled the air, and were not stilled until some one arose and announced that the president-elect was not in the hall. Paul, after a glance of bewilderment at Neil, had sat silent in his chair with something between a sneer and a scowl on his face. Now he jumped up.

"Come on; let's get out of here," he muttered. "They act like a lot of idiots." Neil followed, and they found themselves in a pushing throng at the door. The chairman was vainly clamoring for some one to put a motion to adjourn, but none heeded him. The crowd pushed and shoved, but made no progress.

"Open that door," cried Paul.

"Try it yourself," answered a voice up front. "It's locked!"

A murmur arose that quickly gave place to cries of wrath and indignation. "The sophs did it!" "Where are they?" "Break the door down!" Those at the rear heaved and pushed.

"Stop shoving, back there!" yelled those in front. "You're squashing us flat."

"Everybody away from the door!" shouted Neil. "Let's see if we can't get it open." The fellows finally fell back to some extent, and Neil, Paul, and some of the others examined the lock. The key was still there, but, unfortunately, on the outside. Breaking the door down was utterly out of the question, since it was of solid oak and several inches thick. The self-appointed committee shook its several heads.

"We'll have to yell for the janitor," said Neil. "Where does he hang out?"

But none knew. Neil went to one of the three windows and

Ralph Henry Barbour

raised it. Instantly a chorus of derision floated up from below. Gathered almost under the windows was a throng of sophomores, their upturned faces just visible in the darkness.

"O Fresh! O Fresh!" "Want to come down?" "Why don't you jump?" These gibes were followed by cheers for "'04" and loud groans. Neil turned and faced his angry classmates.

"Look here, fellows," he said, "we don't want to have to yell for the janitor with those sophs there; that's too babyish. The key's in the outside of the lock. I think I can get down all right by the ivy, and I'll unlock the door if those sophs will let me. If two or three of you will follow I guess we can do it all right."

"Bully for you!" "Plucky boy!" cried the audience. But for a moment none came forward to share the risk. Then Paul pushed his way to the window.

"Here, I'll go with you, chum," he said, with a suggestion of swagger. "We can manage those dubs down there alone. The rest of you can sit down and tell stories; we'll let you out in a minute," he added scathingly.

"That's Gale," whispered some one. "Fresh kid!", added another angrily. But the gibe had the desired effect. Four other freshmen signified their willingness to die for their class, and Neil climbed on to the broad window-sill. His reappearance was the signal for another outburst from the watching sophomores.

"Don't jump, sonny; you may hurt yourself." "He's going to fly, fellows! Good little Freshie's got wings!" "Say, we'll let you out in the morning! Good-night!"

But when Neil, divesting himself of coat and shoes, swung out and laid hold of the largest of the big ivy branches that clung there to the wall, the jeers died away. The hall where the meeting had been held was on the third floor, and when Neil stepped from the window-sill he hung fully twenty-five feet from the ground. The ivy branch, ages old, was almost as large as his wrist, and quite strong enough to bear his weight just as long as it did not tear from its fastenings. Whether it would hold in place remained to be seen. Neil judged that if he could lower himself fifteen feet by its aid he could easily drop the rest of the distance without injury. The window above was black with watchers as he began his journey, and many voices cheered him on. Paul, his feet hanging over the black void, sat on the narrow ledge and waited his turn.

"Go fast, chum," he counseled, "but don't lose your grip. I'll wait until you're down."

"All right," answered Neil. Then, with a great rustling of the thick-growing leaves, he lowered himself by arm's lengths. The vine swayed and gave at every strain, but held. From below came the sound of clapping. Hand under hand he went. The oblong of faint light above receded fast. His stockinged feet gripped the vine tightly. In the group of sophomores the clapping grew into cheers.

"Good work, Freshie!" "You're all right!"

Then, with the ground almost at his feet, Neil let go and dropped lightly into a bed of shrubbery. The fellows above applauded wildly. With a glance at the near-by group of sophomores, Neil ran. Several of the enemy started to intercept him, but were called back.

"Let him go! He's all right! We've had our fun!" And Neil sprang up the steps and into the building without molestation. Meanwhile Paul was making his descent and receiving his meed of applause from friend and foe. And as he dropped to earth there came a sound of cheering from the building, and the freshmen, released by the unlocking of the door, emerged on to the steps and path.

"Five this way!" was the cry. "Rush the sophs!"

Ralph Henry Barbour

But wiser counsels prevailed and, each cheering loudly, the representatives of the rival classes took themselves off.

Neil and Paul were the last to leave the building, since they had been obliged to return to the room for their shoes and coats. Paul had forgotten some of his disappointment during the later proceedings, and appeared very well satisfied with himself.

"We showed them what Hillton chaps can do, chum," he said. "And I'll bet they'll regret electing that fellow Livingston before I'm through with them! Much I care about their old presidency! They're a pack of silly little kids, any way. Let's go to bed."

CHAPTER VI

MILLS, HEAD COACH

"TO THE IN-FANTS OF 1905:

"GREETING!

"The class of 1904, an-i-mat-ed by the kind-li-est of sen-ti-ments, has, at an ex-pen-se of much time and thought, form-u-lat-ed the fol-low-ing RULES for the guid-ance of your todd-ling foot-steps at this the out-set of your col-lege car-eers. A strict ad-her-ence to these PRE-CEPTS will in-sure to you the ad-mi-ra-tion of your fond par-ents, the re-spect of your friends, and the love of the SOPH-O-MORE CLASS, which, in the ab-sence of rel-at-ives, will, with thought-ful, tender care, stand ever by to guard you from the world's hard knocks.

"ATTEND, INFANTS!

"1. R-spect for eld-ers and those in auth-or-ity is one of child-hood's most charm-ing traits. There-for take off your hat to all SOPH-O-MORES, and when in their pres-ence al-ways main-tain a def-er-en-tial sil-ence.

"2. Tall hats and canes as art-i-cles of child-ren's attire are ex-treme-ly un-be-com-ing, and are there-for strict-ly pro-hib-it-ed.

"3. Smok-ing, either of pipes, cig-ars, or cig-ar-ettes, stunts the growth and re-tards the dev-el-op-ment of in-tel-lect. Child-ren, be-ware!

"4. A suf-fic-ien-cy of sleep and plain, whole-some fare are strong-ly re-com-mend-ed.

"Early to bed and early to rise
Makes little Freshie healthy and wise.

"Avoid late hours and rich food, es-pec-ial-ly fudge.

"5. That you may not be tempt-ed to trans-gress the pre-ceed-ing rule, it has been thought best to pro-hib-it the Freshman Din-ner, which in pre-vi-ous years has ruin-ed so many young lives. The hab-it of hold-ing these din-ners is a per-nic-ious one and must be stamp-ed out. To this end the CLASS OF 1904 will ex-ert its strong-est ef-forts, and you are here-by warn-ed that any at-tempt to re-vive this lam-ent-able cust-om will bring down up-on you severe chast-ise-ment.

"We must be cruel only to be kind;
Pause and reflect, who would be dined.

"Heed and prof-it by these PRE-CEPTS, dear child-ren, that you may grow up to be great and noble men like those who sub-scribe them-selves,

"Pa-ter-nal-ly yours,

"THE CLASS OF 1904.

"You are ad-ver-tis-ed by your lov-ing friends."

This startling information, printed in sophomore red on big white placards, flamed from every available space in and about the campus the next morning. The nocturnal bill-posters had shown themselves no respecters of places, for the placards adorned not fences and walls alone, but were pasted on the granite steps of each recitation hall. All the forenoon groups of staid seniors, grinning juniors and sophomores, or vexed freshmen stood in front of the placards and read the inscriptions with varied emotions. But in the afternoon a cheering mob of the "infants" marched through the college and town and tore down or effaced every poster they could find. But they didn't get as far from the campus as the athletic field, and so it was not until Neil and Paul and one or two other freshmen reported for practise at four o'clock that it was discovered that the high board fence surrounding the field was a mass of the objectionable signs from end to end.

"Oh, let them stay," said Neil. "I think they're rather funny myself. And as for their stopping the freshman dinner, why we'll wait and see. If they try it we'll have our chance to get back at them."

"R-r-revenge!" muttered South, who, with a lacrosse stick over his shoulder and an attire consisting wholly of a pair of flapping white trunks, a faded green shirt, and a pair of canvas shoes, had come out to join the lacrosse candidates.

"King suggested our getting some small posters printed in blue with just the figures "05" on them, and pasting one on every soph's window," said Paul, "but Livingston wouldn't hear of it. I think it would be a good game, eh?"

"Faculty'd kick up no end of a rumpus," said South.

"I haven't heard that they are doing much about these things," answered Paul. "If the sophs can stick things around why can't we?"

"You'd better ask the Dean," suggested Neil. "Hello, who's that chap?"

They had entered the grounds and were standing on the steps of the locker-house. The person to whom Neil referred was just coming through the gate. He was a medium-sized man of about thirty years, with a good-looking, albeit very freckled face, and a good deal of sandy hair. The afternoon was quite warm, and he carried his straw hat in one very brown hand, while over his arm lay a sweater of Erskine purple, a pair of canvas trousers, and two worn shoes.

"Blessed if I know who he is!" murmured South. They watched the newcomer as he traversed the path and reached the steps. As he passed them and entered the building he looked them over keenly with a pair of very sharp and very light blue eyes.

"Wow!" muttered Paul. "He looked as though he was trying to decide whether I would taste better fried or baked."

"I wonder -" began Neil. But at that moment Tom Cowan came up and Paul put the question to him.

"The fellow that just came in?" repeated Cowan. "That, my boy, is a gentleman who will have you standing on your head in just about twenty minutes. Some eight or ten years ago he was popularly known hereabouts as 'Whitey' Mills. To-day, if you know your business, you'll address him as *Mister* Mills."

"Oh," said Neil, "he's the head coach, is he?"

"He is, my young friend. And as he used to be one of the finest half-backs in the country, I guess you'll see something of him before you make the team. I dare say he can teach even you something about playing your position." Cowan grinned and passed on.

"Oh, go to thunder!" muttered Neil, following him into the building.

He found Mills being introduced by Devoe to such of the new candidates as were on hand.

"You remember Cowan, I guess," Devoe was saying. "He played right-guard last year." Mills and Cowan shook hands.

"And this is Fletcher, a new man," continued the captain, "and Gale, too; they're both Hillton fellows and played at half. It was Fletcher that made that fine run in the St. Eustace game. Gale was the captain last year."

Mills shook hands with each, but beyond a short nod of his head and a brief "Glad to meet you," displayed no knowledge of their fame.

"Grouchy chap," commented Paul when, the coach out of hearing, they were changing their clothes.

"Well, he doesn't hurt himself talking," answered Neil. "But he looks as though he knew his business. His eyes are like little blue-steel gimlets."

"Doesn't look much for strength, though," said Paul.

But when, a few minutes later, Mills appeared on the gridiron in football togs, Paul was forced to alter his opinion. Chest, arms, and legs were a mass of muscle, and the head coach looked as though he could render a good account of himself against the stiffest line that could be put together.

The practise began with ten minutes of falling on the ball. The candidates were lined out in two strings across the field, the old men in one, the new material in another. Neil and Paul were among the latter, and Mills held their ball. Standing at the right end of the line, he rolled the pigskin in front of and slightly away from the line, and one after another the men leaped forward and flung themselves upon it, missing it at first as often as not, and rolling about on the turf as though suddenly seized with fits. Neil rather prided himself on his ability to fall on the ball, and went at it like an old stager, or so he thought. But if he expected commendation he found none. When the last man had rolled around after the elusive pigskin, Mills went to the otherend of the line and did it all over again.

When it came Neil's turn he plunged out, found the ball

Ralph Henry Barbour

nicely, and snuggled it against his breast. To his surprise when he arose Mills left his place and walked out to him.

"Let's try that again," he said. Neil tossed him the ball and went back to his place. Mills nodded to him and rolled the pigskin toward him. Neil dropped on his hip, securing the ball under his right arm. Like a flash Mills was over him, and with a quick blow of his hand had sent the leather bobbing across the turf yards away.

"When you get it, hold on to it," he said dryly. Neil arose with reddening cheeks and, amid the smiles of the others, went back to his place trying to decide whether, if he could have his way, the coach should perish by boiling oil or by merely being drawn and quartered. But after that it was a noticeable fact that the men clung to the ball when they got it as though it were a dearly loved friend.

Later, passing down the line in front from end to end, the head coach threw the ball swiftly at the feet of one after another of the candidates, and each was obliged to drop where he stood and have the ball in his arms when he landed. When Mills came to Neil the latter was still nursing his resentment, and his cheeks still proclaimed that fact. After the boy had dropped on the ball and had tossed it back to the coach their eyes met. In the coach's was just the merest twinkle, a very ghost of a smile; but Neil saw it, and it said to him as plainly as words could have said, "I know just how you feel, my boy, but you'll get over it after a while."

The coach passed on and the flush faded from Neil's cheeks; he even smiled a little. It was all right; Mills understood. It was almost as though they shared a secret between them. Alfred Mills, head football coach at Erskine College, had no more devoted admirer and partizan from that moment than Neil Fletcher, '05.

Next the men were spread out until there was a little space between each, and the coach passed behind the line and shot the ball through, and they had an opportunity to see what they could do with a pigskin that sped away ahead of them. By careful management it is possible in falling on a football to bring almost every portion of the anatomy in violent contact with the ground, and this fact was forcibly brought home to Neil, Paul, and all the others by the time the work was at an end.

"I've got bones I never knew the existence of before," mourned Neil.

"Me too," growled Paul. "And half a dozen of my front teeth are aching from trying to bite holes in the ground; I think they're all loose. If they come out I'll send the dentist's bill to the management."

A few minutes later Neil found himself at left half in one of the six squads of eleven men each that practised advancing the ball. They lined up in ordinary formation, and the ball was passed to one back after another for end runs. Mills went from squad to squad, criticizing briefly and succinctly.

"Don't wait for the quarter to pass," he told Paul, who was playing beside Neil. "On your toes and run hard. Have confidence in your quarter. If the ball isn't ready for you it's not your fault. Try that again."

And when Paul and Neil and the full-back had plowed round the left end once more -

"Quarter, don't hold that ball as though your hand was frozen; keep your hand limber and see that you get the belly of the ball in it, not one end; then it won't tilt itself out. When you get the ball from center rise quickly, put your back against guard, and throw your weight there. And it's just as necessary for you to have confidence in the runner as it is for him to have faith in you. Don't fear that you'll be too quick for him; don't doubt but that he'll be there at the right instant. Keep that in mind and you'll soon have things going like clock-work. Now

Ralph Henry Barbour

once more; ball to left half for a run around right end."

When practise was over that day the new candidates were unanimous in the opinion that they had learned more that afternoon under Mills than they had learned during the whole previous week. Neil, Paul, and Cowan walked back to college together.

"Yes, he's a great little coach," said Cowan, "and a nice chap when you get to know him; no frills on him, you know. And he's plumb full of pluck. They say that once when he played here at half-back he got the ball on Robinson's forty yards and walked down the field and over the line for a touch-down with half the Robinson team hanging on to his legs, and said afterward that he thought he *had* felt some one tugging at him!" Neil laughed.

"But he doesn't look so awfully strong," he objected.

"Well, I guess he was in better trim then," answered Cowan. "Besides, he's built well, you see - most of his weight below his waist; when a chap's that way it's hard to pull him over. I remember last year in the game with Erstham I got through their tackle on a guard-back play, and -"

But Neil had already heard that story of heroic deeds, and so lent a deaf ear to Cowan's boasting. When they reached Main Street a window full of the first issue of the college weekly, The Erskine Purple, met their sight, and they went in and bought copies. On the steps of the laboratory building they opened the inky-smelling journals and glanced through them.

"Here's an account of last night's election," said Cowan. "That's quick work, isn't it? And you can read all about Livingston's brilliant career, Gale. By the way, have you met him yet?"

Paul shook his head. "No, and I'm bearing up under it as well as can be expected."

"You're not missing much," said Cowan. "Hello, here's the football schedule! Want to hear it?" Paul said he did, Neil muttered something unintelligible, and Cowan read as follows:

"E.C.F.B.A.

"SCHEDULE OF GAMES

"Oct. 12. Woodby at Centerport.
  " 16. Dexter at Centerport.
  " 23. Harvard at Cambridge.
  " 26. Erstham at Centerport.
Nov. 2. State University at Centerport.
  " 6. Arrowden at Centerport.
  " 9. Yale at New Haven.
  " 16. Artmouth at Centerport.
  " 23. Robinson at Centerport."

"By Jove!" said Cowan. "We've got seven home games this year! That's fine, isn't it? But I'll bet we'll find Woodby a tough proposition on the 12th. Last year we played her about the 1st of November, and she didn't do a thing to us. And look at the game they've got scheduled for a week before the Robinson game! That'll wear us out; Artmouth will put just about half of our men on the sick-list. And - Hello!" he said, dropping his voice; "talk of an angel!"

A youth of apparently nineteen years was approaching them. He was of moderate height, rather slimly built, with dark eyes and hair, and clean-cut features. He swung a note-book in one hand, and was evidently in deep thought, for he failed to see the group on the steps, and would have passed without speaking had not Cowan called to him. Housed from his reverie, Fanwell Livingston glanced up, and, after nodding to Cowan and Neil, turned in at the gate.

"I suppose you want congratulations," said Cowan. "Well, you can have mine."

"And mine," added Neil. "And Gale here will extend his as soon as he's properly introduced. Mr. Gale - Mr. Livingston."

"Victory - Defeat," added Cowan with a grin. The two candidates for the freshman presidency shook hands, Paul without enthusiasm, Livingston heartily.

"Congratulations, of course," murmured the former.

"Thank you," answered the president. "You're very generous. After all, I dare say you've got the best of it, for you'll have the satisfaction of knowing that if the fellows had chosen you you would have done much better than I shall. However, I hope we'll be friends, Mr. Gale." Livingston's smile was undeniably winning, and Paul was forced to return it.

"You're very good," he answered quite affably. "I hope we will." Livingston nodded, smiled again, and turned to Cowan.

"Well, they tell me you fellows are in for desperate deeds this year," he said.

"How's that?" asked Cowan.

"Aren't you in on the sophomore councils? Why, I'm told that if the freshmen don't give up the dinner plan I'm to be kidnaped."

"How'd you hear -" began Cowan. Then he paused with some confusion. "Who told you that rot?" he asked with a laugh.

"Oh, it came in a roundabout way," answered Livingston. "I dare say it's just talk."

"Some freshman nonsense," said Cowan. "I guess we'll do our best to keep you fellows from eating too much, but -" He shrugged his big shoulders. Livingston, observing him shrewdly, began for the first time since intelligence of the supposed project had reached him to give credence to it. But he laughed carelessly as he turned away.

"Oh, well, we have to keep you fellows amused, of course, and if you like to try kidnaping you may."

"I wish the sophs would try it," said Neil warmly. Cowan turned to him.

"Well, if they did - *if* they did - I guess they'd succeed," he drawled.

"Well, if they do - *if* they do," answered Neil, "I'll bet they won't succeed."

"You'd stop us, perhaps?" sneered Cowan.

"Easily," answered Neil, smiling sweetly; "there are only a hundred or so of you."

"There's no one like a week-old freshman for self-importance," Cowan said, laughing in order to hide his vexation.

"Unless it's a third-year sophomore," Neil retorted.

"Oh, well," Paul interposed, "it's all poppycock, anyhow."

"That's all," said Livingston.

"Of course," agreed Cowan.

Neil was silent.

Ralph Henry Barbour

CHAPTER VII

THE GENTLE ART OF HANDLING PUNTS

Life now was filled with hard work for both Neil and Paul. Much of the novelty that had at first invested study with an exhilarating interest had worn off, and they had settled down to the daily routine of lectures and recitations just as though they had been Erskine undergrads for years instead of a week. The study and the adjoining bed-room were at last furnished to suit; The First Snow was hung, the "rug for the wash-stand" was in place, and the objectionable towel-rack had given way to a smaller but less erratic affair.

Every afternoon saw the two boys on Erskine Field. Mills was a hard taskmaster, but one that inspired the utmost confidence, and as a result of some ten days' teaching the half hundred candidates who had survived the first weeding-out process were well along in the art of football. The new men were coached daily in the rudiments; were taught to punt and catch, to fall on the ball, to pass without fumbling, to start quickly, and to run hard. Exercise in the gymnasium still went on, but the original twenty-minute period had gradually diminished to ten. Neil and Paul, with certain other candidates for the back-field, were daily instructed in catching punts and forming interference. Every afternoon the practise was watched by a throng of students who were quick to applaud good work, and whose presence was a constant incentive to the players. There was a strong sentiment throughout the college in favor of leaving nothing undone that might secure a victory over

Robinson. The defeat of the previous year rankled, and Erskine was grimly determined to square accounts with her lifelong rival. As one important means to this end the college was searched through and through for heavy material, for Robinson always turned out teams that, whatever might be their playing power, were beef and brawn from left end to right. And so at Erskine men who didn't know a football from a goal-post were hauled from studious retirement simply because they had weight and promised strength, and were duly tried and, usually, found wanting. One lucky find, however, rewarded the search, a two-hundred-pound sophomore named Browning, who, handicapped at the start with a colossal ignorance regarding all things pertaining to the gridiron, learned with wonderful rapidity, and gave every promise of turning himself into a phenomenal guard or tackle.

On the 5th of October a varsity and a second squad were formed, and Neil and Paul found themselves at left and right half respectively on the latter. Cowan was back at right-guard on the varsity, a position which he had played satisfactorily the year before. Neil had already made the discovery that he had, despite his Hillton experience, not a little to learn, and he set about learning it eagerly. Paul made the same discovery, but, unfortunately for himself, the discovery wounded his pride, and he accepted the criticisms of coach and captain with rather ill grace.

"That dub Devoe makes me very weary," he confided to Neil one afternoon. "He thinks he knows it all and no one else has any sense."

"He doesn't strike me that way," answered his chum. "And I think he does know a good deal of football."

"You always stick up for him," growled Paul. "And for Mills, too - white-haired, freckle-faced chump!"

"Don't be an idiot," said Neil. "One's captain and t'other is coach, and they're going to rub it into us whenever they please, and the best thing for us to do is to take it and look cheerful."

"That's it; we *have* to take it," Paul objected. "They can put us on the bench if they want to and keep us there all the season; I know that. But, just the same, I don't intend to lick Devoe's boots or rub my head in the dirt whenever Mills looks at me."

"Well, it looks to me as though you'd been rubbing your head in the dirt already," laughed Neil.

"Connor stepped on me there," muttered Paul, wiping a clump of mud from his forehead. "Come on; Mills is yelling for us. More catching punts, I suppose."

And his supposition was correct. Across the width of the sunlit field Graham, the two-hundred-and-thirty-pound center rush, stooped over the pigskin. Beside him were two pairs of end rushes, and behind him, with outstretched hands, stood Ted Foster. Foster gave a signal, the ball went back to him on a long pass, and he sent it over the gridiron toward where Neil, Paul, and two other backs were waiting. The ends came down under the kick, the ball thumped into Paul's hands, Neil and another formed speedy interference, and the three were well off before the ends, like miniature cyclones, were upon them and had dragged Paul to earth.

The head coach, a short but sturdy figure in worn-out trousers and faded purple shirt, stood on the edge of the cinder track and viewed the work with critical eye. When the ends had trotted back over the field with the ball to repeat the proceeding, he made himself heard:

"Spread out more, fellows, and don't all stand in a line across the field. You've got to learn now to judge kicks; you can't expect to always find yourself just under them. Fletcher, as soon as you've decided who is to take the ball yell out. Then play to the runner; every other man form into interference and get him up the field. Now then! Play quick!"

The ball was in flight again, and once more the ends were speeding across under it. "Mine!" cried Neil. Then the leather was against his breast and he was dodging forward, Paul ahead of him to bowl over opposing players, and Pearse, a full-back candidate, plunging along beside. One - two - three of the ends were passed, and the ball had been run back ten yards. Then Stone, last year's varsity left end, fooled Paul, and getting inside him, nailed Neil by the hips.

"Well tackled, Stone," called Mills. "Gale, you were asleep, man; Stone ought never to have got through there. Fletcher, you're going to lose the ball some time when you need it badly if you don't catch better than that. Never reach up for it; remember that your opponent can't tackle you until you've touched it; wait until it hits against your stomach, and then grip it hard. If you take it in the air it's an easy stunt for an opponent to knock it out of your hands; but if you've got it hugged against your body it won't matter how hard you're thrown, the ball's yours for keeps. Bear that in mind."

On the next kick Neil called to Gale to take the pigskin. Paul misjudged it, and was forced to turn and run back. He missed the catch, a difficult one under the circumstances, and also missed the rebound. By this time the opposing ends were down on him. The ball trickled across the running track, and Paul stooped to pick it up. But Stone was ahead of him, and seizing the pigskin, was off for what would have been a touch-down had it been in a game.

"What's the matter, Gale?" cried Mills angrily. "Why didn't you fall on that ball?"

"It was on the cinders," answered Paul, in evident surprise. Mills made a motion of disgust, of tragic impatience.

"I don't care," he cried, "if it was on broken glass! You've got orders to fall on the ball. Now bring it over here, put it down and - *fall - on - it*!"

Neil watched his chum apprehensively. Knowing well Paul's impatience under discipline, he feared that the latter would give way to anger and mutiny on the spot. But Paul did as directed, though with bad grace, and contented himself with muttered words as he threw the pigskin to a waiting end and went back to his place.

Soon afterward they were called away for a ten-minute line-up. Paul, still smarting under what in his own mind he termed a cruel indignity, played poorly, and ere the ten minutes was half up was relegated to the benches, his place at right half being taken by Kirk. The second managed to hold the varsity down to one score that day, and might have taken the ball over itself had not Pearse fumbled on the varsity's three yards. As it was, they were given a hearty cheer by the watchers when time was called, and they trotted to the bucket to be sponged off. Then those who had not already been in the line-up were given the gridiron, and the varsity and second were sent for a trot four times around the field, the watchful eye of "Baldy" Simson, Erskine's veteran trainer, keeping them under surveillance until they had completed their task and had trailed out the gate toward the locker-house, baths, and rub-downs.

CHAPTER VIII

THE KIDNAPING

Fanwell Livingston was curled in the window-seat in his front room, his book close to the bleared pane, striving to find light enough by which to study. Outside it was raining in a weary, desultory way, and the heavens were leaden-hued. Livingston's quarters were on the front of that big lemon-yellow house at the corner of Oak and King Streets, about equidistant from campus and field. The outlook to-day was far from inspiriting. When he raised his eyes from the pages before him he saw an empty road running with water; beyond that a bare, weed-grown, sodden field that stretched westward to the unattractive backs of the one-and two-storied shops on Main Street. Livingston's room wasn't in any sense central, but he liked it because it was quiet, because aside from the family he had the house to himself, and because Mrs. Saunders, his landlady, was goodness itself and administered to his comfort almost as his own mother would have done.

The freshman president laid aside his book, grimaced at the dreary prospect, and took out his watch. "Ten minutes after five," he murmured. "Heavens, what a beastly dark day! I'll have to start to get dressed before long. Too bad we've got such weather for the affair." He glanced irresolutely toward the gas-fixture, and from thence to where his evening clothes lay spread out on the couch. For it was the evening of the Freshman Class Dinner. While he was striving to find energy wherewith to tear himself from the soft cushions and make a

Ralph Henry Barbour

light, footsteps sounded outside his door, and some one demanded admission.

"Come in!" he called.

The door swung open, was closed swiftly and softly again, and Neil Fletcher crossed the room. He looked rather like a tramp; his hat was a misshapen thing of felt from which the water dripped steadily as he tossed it aside; his sweater - he wore no coat - was soaking wet; and his trousers and much-darned golf stockings were in scarcely better condition. His hair looked as though he had just taken his head from a water-bucket, and his face bespoke excitement.

"They're coming after you, Livingston," he cried in an intense whisper. "I heard Cowan telling Carey in the locker-room a minute ago; they didn't know I was there; it was dark as dark. They've got a carriage, and there are going to be nearly a dozen of them. I ran all the way as soon as I got on to Oak Street. There wasn't time to get any of the fellows together, so I just sneaked right over here. You can get out now and go - some-where - to our room or the library. They won't look for you there, eh? There's a fellow at the corner watching, but I don't think he saw me, and I can settle with him; or maybe you could get out the back way and double round by the railroad? You can't stay here, because they're coming right away; Cowan said -"

"For heaven's sake, Fletcher, what do you mean?" asked Livingston. "You don't want me to believe that they're really going to run off with me?"

Neil, gasping for breath, subsided on to the window-seat and nodded his head vigorously. "That's just what I do mean. There's no doubt about it, my friend. Didn't I tell you I heard Cowan -"

"Oh, Cowan!"

"I know, but it was all in earnest. Carey and he are on their way to Pike's stable for the carriage, and the others are to meet there. They've had fellows watching you all day. There's one at the corner now - a tall, long-nosed chap that I've seen in class. So get your things and get out as soon as you can move."

Livingston, with his hands in his pockets, stared thoughtfully out of the window, Neil watching him impatiently and listening apprehensively for the sound of carriage wheels down the street.

"It doesn't seem to me that they could be idiots enough to attempt such a silly trick," said Livingston at last. "You - you're quite sure you weren't mistaken - that they weren't stringing you?"

"They didn't know I was there!" cried Neil in exasperation. "I went in late - Mills had us blocking kicks - and was changing my things over in a dark corner when they hurried in and went over into the next alley and began to talk. At first they were whispering, but after a bit they talked loud enough for me to hear every word."

"Well, anyhow - and I'm awfully much obliged, Fletcher - I don't intend to run from a few sophs. I'll lock the front door and this one and let them hammer."

"But -"

"Nonsense; when they find they can't get in they'll get tired and go away."

"And you'll go out and get nabbed at the corner! That's a clever program, I don't think!" cried Neil in intense scorn. "Now you listen to me, Livingston. What you want to do is to put your glad rags in a bag and - What's that?"

He leaped to his feet and peered out of the window. Just within his range of vision a carriage, drawn by two dripping, sorry-looking nags, drew up under the slight shelter of an elm-tree about fifty yards away from the house. From it emerged eight fellows in rain-coats, while the tall, long-nosed watcher whom Neil had seen at the corner joined them and made his report. The group looked toward Livingston's window and Neil dodged back.

"It's too late now," he whispered. "There they are."

"Look a bit damp, don't they," laughed Livingston softly as he peered out over the other's shoulder. "I'll go down and lock the door."

"No, stay here," said Neil. "I'll look after that; they might get you. I wish it wasn't so dark! How about the back way? Can't you get out there and sneak around by the field?"

"I told you I wasn't going to run away from them," replied his host, "and I haven't changed my mind."

"You're an obstinate ass!" answered Neil. He scowled at the calm and smiling countenance of the freshman president a moment, and then turned quickly and pulled the shades at the windows. "I've got it!" he cried. "Look here, will you do as I tell you? If you do I promise you we'll fool them finely."

"I'm not going out of this room," objected Livingston.

"Yes, you are - into the next one. And you're going to lock the door behind you; and I'm going to look after our sophomore callers. Now go ahead. Do as I tell you, or I'll go off and leave you to be eaten alive!" Neil, grinning delightedly, thrust the unwilling Livingston before him. "Now lock the door and keep quiet. No matter what you hear, keep quiet and stay in there."

"But -"

"You be hanged!" Neil pulled to the bed-room door, and

listened until he heard the key turn on the other side. Then he stole to the window and, lifting a corner of the shade, peeped out. The group of sophomores were no longer in sight, but at that moment he heard the front door close softly. There was no time to lose. He found a match and hurriedly lighted one burner over the study table. Then, turning it down to a mere blue point of light, he flung himself back among the cushions on the window-seat, and with a heart that hammered violently at his ribs waited.

Almost in the next moment there were sounds of shuffling feet outside the study door, a low voice, and then a knock. Neil took a long breath.

"Come in," he called drowsily.

The door opened. Neil arose and walked to the gas-fixture, knocking over a chair on his way.

"Come in, whoever you are," he muttered. "Guess I was almost asleep." He reached up a hand and turned out the gas. The room, almost dark before, was now blackness from wall to wall. "Pshaw," said Neil, "I've turned the pesky thing out! Just stand still until I find a match or you'll break your shins." He groped his way toward the mantel. Now was the sophomores' opportunity, and they seized it. Neil had done his best to imitate Livingston's careful and rather precise manner of speaking, and the invaders, few of whom even knew the president of the freshman class by sight, never for an instant doubted that they had captured him.

Neil found himself suddenly seized by strong arms. With a cry of simulated surprise, he struggled feebly.

"Here, what's up, fellows?" he remonstrated. "Look out, I tell you! *Don't do that!*"

Then he was borne, protesting and kicking, feet foremost, through the door, out into the hall and down the stairs. When the front door was thrown open Neil was alarmed to find that although almost dark it was still light enough for his captors to discover their mistake. Hiding his face as best he could, he lifted his voice in loud cries for help. It worked like a charm. Instantly a carriage robe was thrown over his head and he was hurried down the steps, across the muddy sidewalk, and into the waiting vehicle which had been driven up before the house. Once inside, Neil was safe from detection, for the hack, the shades drawn up before the windows, was as dark as Egypt. Neil sighed his relief, muttered a few perfunctory threats from behind the uncomfortable folds of the ill-smelling robe, and, with one fellow sitting on his chest and three others holding his legs, felt the carriage start.

Despite the enveloping folds about his head he could hear quite well; hear the horses' feet go *squish-squash* in the mud; hear the carriage creak on its aged hinges; hear the shriek of a distant locomotive as they approached the railroad. His captors were congratulating themselves on the success of their venture.

"Easier than I thought it'd be," said one, and at the reply Neil figuratively pricked up his ears.

"Pshaw, I knew we'd have no trouble; Livingston was so cock-sure that we wouldn't try it that he'd probably forgotten all about it. I guess that conceited little fool Fletcher will talk out of the other side of his mouth for a while now. What do you think? He had the nerve to tell me last week that he guessed *he* could prevent a kidnaping, as there were only about a hundred of us sophs!"

The others laughed.

"Well, he is a chesty young kid, isn't he?" asked a third speaker. "I guess it's just as well we didn't have to kidnap *him*, eh? By the way, our friend here seems ill at ease. Maybe we'd better get off of him now and give him a breath of air. We don't want a corpse on our hands."

The sophomores found seats and the robe was unwound from about Neil's head, much to that youth's delight. He took a good long breath and, grinning enjoyably in the darkness, settled himself to make the best of his predicament. Now that he had discovered Tom Cowan to be one of his abductors, he was filled with such glee that he found it hard work to keep silent. But he did, and all the gibes of his captors, uttered in quite the most polite language imaginable, failed to elicit a reply.

"Beautiful evening for a drive, is it not?" asked one.

"I trust you had not planned to attend the freshman dinner to-night?" asked another. "For I fear we shall be late in reaching home."

"You are quite comfortable? Is there any particular road you would like to drive? any part of our lovely suburbs you care to visit?"

"Surly brute!" growled a fourth, who was Cowan. "Let's make him speak, eh? Let's twist his arm a bit."

"You sit still or I'll punch your thick head," said the first speaker coldly. "What I dislike about you, Cowan, is that you are never able to forget that you're a mucker. I wish you'd try," he continued wearily, "it's so monotonous."

Cowan was silent an instant; then laughed uncertainly.

"I suppose you fancy you're a wit, Baker," he said, "but I think you're mighty tiresome."

"Don't let it trouble you," was the calm reply. Some one laughed drowsily. Then there was silence save for the sound of the horses' feet, the complaining of the well-worn hack and the occasional voice of the driver outside on the box. Neil began to feel rather drowsy himself; the motion was lulling, and now that they had crossed the railroad-track and reached the turnpike along the river, the carriage traveled smoothly. It was black night outside now, and through the nearest window at which the curtain had been lowered Neil could see nothing save an occasional light in some house. He didn't know where he was being taken, and didn't much care. They rolled steadily on for half an hour longer, during which time two at least of his captors proclaimed their contentment by loud snoring. Then the carriage slowed down, the sleeping ones were awakened, and a moment later a flood of light entering the window told Neil that the journey was at an end.

"Far as we go," said some one. "All out here and take the car ahead!" A door was opened, two of his captors got out, and Neil was politely invited to follow. He did so. Before him was the open door of a farm-house from which the light streamed hospitably. It was still drizzling, and Neil took shelter on the porch unchallenged; now that the abductors had got him some five miles from Centerport, they were not so attentive. The others came up the steps and the carriage was led away toward the barn.

"If your Excellency will have the kindness to enter the house," said Baker, with low obeisance, "he will find accommodations which, while far from befitting your Excellency's dignity, are, unfortunately, the best at our command."

Neil accepted the invitation silently, and entering the doorway, found himself in a well-lighted room wherein a table was set for supper. The others followed, Cowan grinning from ear to ear in anticipation of the victim's discomfiture. In his eagerness he was the first to catch sight of Neil's face. With a howl of surprise he sprang back, almost upsetting Baker.

"What's the matter with you?" cried the latter. Cowan made no answer, but stared stupidly at Neil.

"Eh? What?" Baker sprang forward and wheeled their victim into the light. Neil turned and faced them smilingly. The four stared in bewilderment. It was Baker who first found words.

"*Well, I'll - be - hanged!*" he murmured.

Neil turned placidly to the discomfited Cowan.

"You see, Cowan," he said sweetly, "one against a hundred isn't such big odds, after all, is it?"

Ralph Henry Barbour

CHAPTER IX

THE BROKEN TRICYCLE

As soon as Livingston heard the kidnapers staggering downstairs with their burden he unlocked the bed-room door and stole to the window. He saw Neil, his head hidden by the carriage robe, thrust into the hack and driven away, and saw the conspirators for whom the vehicle afforded no room separate and disappear in the gathering darkness. Livingston's emotions were varied: admiration for Neil's harebrained but successful ruse, distaste for the sorry part taken by himself in the affair, and amusement over the coming amazement and discomfiture of the enemy were mingled. In the end delight in the frustration of the sophomores' plan gained the ascendency, and he resolved that although Neil would miss the freshman dinner he should have it made up to him.

And so in his speech an hour or so later Fanwell Livingston told the astonished company of the attempted kidnaping and of its failure, and never before had Odd Fellows' Hall rang with such laughter and cheering. And a little knot of sophomores, already bewildered by the appearance of the freshman president on the scene, were more than ever at a loss. They stood under an awning across the street, some twenty or thirty of them, and asked each other what it meant. Content with the supposed success of the abduction, they had made no attempt to prevent the dinner. And now Livingston, who by every law of nature should be five miles out in the country, was presiding at the feast and moving his audience to the wildest applause.

"But I helped put him in the hack!" Carey cried over and over.

"And I saw it drive off with him!" marveled another.

"And if that's Livingston, where's Baker, and Morton, and Cowan, and Dyer?" asked the rest. And all shook their heads and gazed bewildered through the rain to where a raised window-shade gave them occasional glimpses of "Fan" Livingston, a fine figure in dinner jacket and white shirt bosom, leading the cheering.

"*Rah-rah-rah, Rah-rah-rah, Rah-rah-rah, Fletcher!*"

The group under the awning turned puzzled looks upon each other.

"Who's Fletcher? What are they cheering Fletcher for?" was asked. But none could answer.

But over in the hall it was different. Not a lad there, perhaps, but would have been glad to have exchanged places with the gallant confounder of sophomore plots, who was pictured in most minds as starving to death somewhere out in the rain, a captive in the ungentle hands of the enemy.

However, starving Neil certainly was not. For at that very moment, seated at the hospitable board of Farmer Hutchins, he was helping himself to his fifth hot biscuit, and allowing Miss Hutchins, a red-cheeked and admiring young lady of fourteen years, to fill his teacup for the second time. From the role of prisoner Neil had advanced himself to the position of honored guest. For after the first consternation, bewilderment, and mortification had passed, his captors philosophically accepted the situation, and under the benign influence of cold chicken and hot soda biscuits found themselves not only able to display equanimity, but to join in the laugh against themselves and to admire the cleverness displayed in their outwitting. Of the four sophomores Cowan's laughter and praise alone rang false. But Neil was supremely indifferent to that youth's sentiments. The others he soon discovered to be thoroughly good fellows, and there is no doubt but that he enjoyed the hospitality of Farmer Hutchins more than he would have enjoyed the freshman class dinner.

At nine o'clock the drive back to Centerport began, and as the horses soon found that they were headed toward home the journey occupied surprisingly little time, and at ten Neil was back in his room awaiting the return of Paul. To Neil's surprise that gentleman was at first decidedly grumpy.

"You might have let me into it," he grumbled.

But Neil explained and apologized until at length peace was restored. Then he had to tell Paul all about it from first to last, and Paul laughed until he choked; "I - I just wish - wish I had - seen Cowan's - face when - he - found it - out!" he shrieked.

One result of that night's adventure was that the Class of 1905 was never thereafter bothered in the slightest degree by the sophomores; it appeared to be the generally accepted verdict that the freshmen had established their right to immunity from all molestation. Another result was that Neil became a class hero and a college notable. Younger freshmen pointed him out to each other in admiring awe; older and more influential ones went out of their way to claim recognition from him; sophomores viewed him with more than passing interest, and upper-class men predicted for him a brilliant college career. Even the Dean, when he passed Neil the following afternoon and returned his bow, allowing himself something almost approaching a grin. Neil, however, bore his honors modestly even while acknowledging to himself the benefit of them. He learned that his chances of making a certain society, membership in which was one of his highest ambitions, had been more than doubled, and was glad accordingly. (He was duly elected and underwent rigorous initiation proudly and joyfully.)

The kidnaping affair even affected his football standing, for

Mills and Devoe and Simson, the trainer, spoke or looked applause, while the head coach thereafter displayed quite a personal interest in him. Several days subsequent to the affair Neil was taking dummy practise with the rest of the second eleven. Mills had appropriated the invention of a Harvard trainer, rigging the dummy with hook and eye-bolt, so that when properly tackled the stuffed canvas effigy of a Robinson player became detached from its cable and fell on to the soft loam much after the manner of a human being. But to bring the dummy from the hook necessitated the fiercest of tackling, and many fellows failed at this. To-day Neil was one of this number. Twice the dummy, bearing upon its breast the brown R of Robinson, had sped away on its twenty-foot flight, and twice Neil had thrown himself upon it without bringing it down. As he arose after the second attempt and brushed the soil from his trousers Mills "went for him."

"You're very ladylike, Fletcher, but as this isn't crewel-work or crochet you'll oblige me by being so rude as to bring that dummy off. Now, once more; put some snap into it! Get your hold, find your purchase, and then throw! Just imagine it's a sophomore, please."

The roar of laughter that followed restored some of Neil's confidence, and, whether he deceived himself into momentarily thinking the dummy a sophomore, he tackled finely, brought the canvas figure from the hook, and triumphantly sat on the letter R.

Signal practise followed work at the dummy that afternoon, and last of all the varsity and second teams had their daily line-up. Neil, however, did not get into this. Greatly to his surprise and disappointment McCullough took his place at left half, and Neil sat on the bench and aggrievedly watched the lucky ones peeling off their sweaters in preparation for the fray. But idleness was not to be his portion, for a moment later Mills called to him:

"Here, take this ball, go down there to the fifteen-yard line, and try drop-kicking. Keep a strict count, and let me know how many tries you had and how many times you put it over the goal."

Neil took the ball and trotted off to the scene of his labors, greatly comforted. Kicking goals from the fifteen-yard line didn't sound very difficult, and he set to work resolved to distinguish himself. But drop-kicks were not among Neil's accomplishments, and he soon found that the cross-bar had a way of being in the wrong place at the critical moment. At first it was hard to keep from turning his head to watch the progress of the game, but presently he became absorbed in his work. As a punter he had been somewhat of a success at Hillton, but drop-kicking had been left to the full-back, and consequently it was unaccustomed work. The first five tries went low, and the next four went high enough but wide of the goal. The next one barely cleared the cross-bar, and Neil was hugely tickled. The count was then ten tries and one goal. He got out of the way in order to keep from being ground to pieces by the struggling teams, and while he stood by and watched the varsity make its first touch-down, ruminated sadly upon the report he would have to render to Mills.

But a long acquaintance with footballs had thoroughly dispelled Neil's awe of them, and he returned to his labor determined to better his score. And he did, for when the teams trotted by him on their way off the field and Mills came up, he was able to report 38 tries, of which 12 were goals.

"Not bad," said the coach. "That'll do for to-day. But whenever you find a football, and don't know what to do with it, try drop-kicking. Your punting is very good, and there's no reason why you shouldn't learn to kick from drop or placement as well. Take my advice and put your heart and brain and muscle into it, for, while we've got backs that can buck and hurdle and run, we haven't many that can be depended on to kick a goal, and we'll need them before long."

Neil trotted out to the locker-house with throbbing heart.

Mills had as good as promised him his place. That is, if he could learn to kick goals. The condition didn't trouble Neil, however; he *could* learn to drop-kick and he *would* learn, he told himself exultantly as he panted under the effects of a cold shower-bath. For a moment the wild idea of rising at unchristian hours and practising before chapel occurred to him, but upon maturer thought was given up. No, the only thing to do was to follow Mills's advice: "Put your heart and brain and muscle into it," the coach had said. Neil nodded vigorously and rubbed himself so hard with the towel as to almost take the skin off. He was late in leaving the house that evening, and as all the fellows he knew personally had already taken their departure, he started back toward the campus alone. Near the corner of King Street he glanced up and saw something a short distance ahead that puzzled him. It looked at first like a cluster of bicycles with a single rider. But as the rider was motionless Neil soon came up to him.

On nearer view he saw that the object was in reality a tricycle, and that it held beside the rider a pair of crutches which lay in supports lengthwise along one side. The machine was made to work with the hands instead of the feet, and a bow-shaped piece of steel which fitted around the operator's knee served as steering apparatus. The youth who sat motionless on the seat was a rather pale-faced, frail-looking lad of eighteen years, and it needed no second glance to tell Neil that he was crippled from his waist down. As Neil approached he was pulling the handles to and fro and looking perplexedly at the gear. The tricycle refused to budge.

"I guess you've broken down," said Neil, approaching. "Stay where you are and I'll have a look."

"Thanks, but you needn't bother," said the lad.

But Neil was already on his knees. The trouble was soon found; the chain had broken and for the present was beyond repair.

"But the wheels will go round, just the same," said Neil cheerfully. "Keep your seat and I'll push you back. Where do you room?"

"Walton," was the answer. "But I don't like to bother you, Mr. Fletcher. You see I have my crutches here, and I can get around very well on them."

"Nonsense, there's no use in your walking all the way to Walton. Here, I'll take the chain off and play horse. By the way, how'd you know my name?"

"Oh, every one knows you since that kidnaping business," laughed the other, beginning to forget some of his shyness. "And besides I've heard the coach speak to you at practise."

"Oh," said Neil, who was now walking behind the tricycle and pushing it before him, "then you've been out to the field, eh?"

"Yes, I like to watch practise. I go out very nearly every day."

"Come to think of it, I believe I've seen you there," said Neil. "It's wonderful how you can get around on this machine as you do. Isn't it hard work at times?"

"Rather, on grades, you know. But on smooth roads it goes very easily; besides, I've worked it every day almost for so long that I've got a pretty good muscle now. My father had this one made for me only two months ago to use here at Erskine. The last machine I had was very much heavier and harder to manage."

"I guess being so light has made it weak," said Neil, "or it wouldn't have broken down like this."

"Oh, I fancy that was more my fault than the tricycle's," answered the boy. As Neil was behind him he did not see the smile that accompanied the words.

"Well, I'll take you home and then wheel the thing down to the bicycle repair-shop near the depot, eh?"

"Oh, no, indeed," protested the other. "I'll - I'll have them send up for it. I wouldn't have you go way down there with it for anything."

"Pshaw! that's no walk; besides, if you have them send, it will be some time to-morrow afternoon before you get it back."

"I sha'n't really need it before then," answered the lad earnestly.

"You might," said Neil. There was such a tone of finality in the reply that the boy on the seat yielded, but for an instant drew his face into a pucker of perplexity.

"Thank you," he said; "it's awfully nice of you to take so much trouble."

"I can't see that," Neil replied. "I don't see how I could do any less. By the way, what's your name, if you don't mind?"

"Sydney Burr."

"Burr? That's why you were stuck there up the road," laughed Neil. "We're in the same class, aren't we?"

"Yes."

At the middle entrance of Walton Hall Neil helped Burr on to his crutches, and would have assisted him up the steps had he not objected.

"Please don't," he said, flushing slightly. "I can get up all right; I do it every day. My room's on this floor, too. I'm awfully much obliged to you for what you've done. I wish you'd come and see me some time - No. 3. Do you - do you think you could?"

"Of course," Neil answered heartily, "I'll be glad to. Three, you said? All right. I'll take this nag down to the blacksmith's now and get him reshod. If they can fix him right off I'll bring him back with me. Where do you stable him?"

"The janitor takes it down-stairs somewhere. If I'm not here just give it to him, please. I wish, though, you wouldn't bother about bringing it back."

"I'll ride him back," laughed Neil. "Good-night."

"Good-night. Don't forget you're coming to see me."

Sydney Burr smiled and, turning, climbed the steps with astonishing ease, using his crutches with a dexterity born of many years' dependence upon them. His lower limbs, slender and frail, swung from side to side, mere useless appendages. Neil sighed as he saw his new acquaintance out of sight, and then started on his errand with the tricycle.

"Poor duffer!" he muttered. "And yet he seems cheerful enough, and looks happy. But to think of having to creep round on stilts or pull himself about on this contrivance! I mustn't forget to call on him; I dare say he hasn't many friends. He seems a nice chap, too; and he'd be frightfully good-looking if he wasn't so white."

It was almost dark when he reached the repair-shop near the railroad, and the proprietor, a wizened little bald-headed man, was preparing to go home.

"Can't fix anything to-night," he protested shrilly. "It's too late; come in the morning."

"Well, if you think I'm going to wheel this thing back here to-morrow you've missed your guess," said Neil. "All it needs is to have a chain link welded or glued or something; it won't take five minutes. And the fellow that owns it is a cripple and can't go out until this machine's fixed. Now go ahead, like a good chap; I'll hold your bonnet."

"Eh? What bonnet?" The little man stared perplexedly.

"I meant I'd help," answered Neil unabashed.

"Help! Huh! Lot's of help, you'd be to any one! Well, let's see it." He knelt and inspected the tricycle, grumbling all the while and shaking his head angrily. "Who said it was broke?" he demanded presently. "Queer kind of break; looks like you'd pried the link apart with a cold-chisel."

"Well, I didn't; nor with a hot chisel. Besides, I've just told you it didn't belong to me. Do I look like a cripple?"

"More like a fool," answered the other with a chuckle.

"You're a naughty old man," said Neil sorrowfully, "and if you were my father I'd spank you." The other was too angry to find words, and contented himself with bending back the damaged link and emitting a series of choking sounds which Neil rightly judged to be expressions of displeasure. When the repair was finished he pushed the machine angrily toward the boy.

"Take it and get out," he said.

"Thanks. How much?"

"Fifty cents," was the reply, given with a toothless grin and a chuckle. "Twenty-five cents for the job and twenty-five cents for working after hours."

"Cheap enough," answered Neil, laying a quarter on the bench. "That's for the job; I'll owe you the rest."

When he reached the first corner the proprietor of the repair-shop was still calling him names and shaking his fist in the air.

Ralph Henry Barbour

"Looked just like a he-witch or something," chuckled Neil, as he propelled his steed toward the campus. "Maybe he will put a curse upon me and my right foot will wither up and I won't be able to kick goals!"

CHAPTER X

NEIL MAKES THE VARSITY

On the 12th of October, Woodby College sent a team of light but very fast football players to Erskine with full determination to bring back the pigskin. And it very nearly succeeded. It was the first game of the season for Erskine, but Woodby had already played two, and was consequently rather more hardened. The first half ended with the score 6 to 6, and the spectators, fully three hundred supporters of the Purple, looked glum. Neil and Paul were given their chance in the second half, taking the places of Gillam and Smith. Many other changes were made, among them one which installed the newly discovered Browning at left guard vice Carey, removed to the bench.

There was no use in attempting to disguise the fact that Woodby literally played all around the home team. Her backs gained almost at will on end runs, and her punting was immeasurably superior. Foster, the Erskine quarter-back, sent kick after kick high into the air, and twenty yards was his best performance. On defense Woodby was almost equally strong, and had Erskine not outweighted her in the line some five pounds per man, would have forced her to kick every time. As it was, the purple-clad backs made but small and infrequent gains through the line, and very shortly found that runs outside of tackle or end were her best cards, even though, as was several times the case, her runners were nailed back of her line for losses.

Ralph Henry Barbour

Team play was as yet utterly lacking in the Erskine eleven, and though the men were as a rule individually brilliant or decidedly promising, Woodby had far the best of it there. Fumbles were many on both sides, but Erskine's were the most costly. Stone's fumble of a free kick soon after the second half began gave Woodby her second touch-down, from which, luckily, she failed to kick goal. The veterans on the team, Tucker at left tackle, Graham at center, Cowan at right-guard, Foster at quarter, and Devoe at right end, played well with the glaring exception of Cowan, whose work in the second half especially was so slipshod that Mills, with wrath in his eye, took him out and put in Bell, a second eleven man.

With the score 11 to 6 against her, Erskine braced up and fought doggedly to score. Neil proved the best ground-gainer, and made several five-and ten-yard runs around right end. Once, with the ball on Woodby's twelve yards and the audience shouting vehemently for a touch-down, Foster called on Paul for a plunge through right tackle. Paul made two yards, but in some manner lost the ball, a fumble that put Erskine back on her fifty-yard line and that sent her hopes of tying the score down to zero.

The second half was to be but fifteen minutes long, and fully ten of the fifteen had gone by when Erskine took up her journey toward Woodby's goal again. Mason, the full-back, and Neil were sent plunging, bucking, hurdling at the enemy's breastworks, and time after time just managed to gain their distance in the three downs. Fortune was favoring Erskine, and Woodby's lighter men were slower and slower in finding their positions after each pile-up. Then, with the pigskin on Woodby's twenty-eight yards, Neil was given the ball for a try outside of right tackle, and by brilliantly leaving his interference, which had become badly tangled up, got safely away and staggered over the line just at the corner. The punt-out was a success and Devoe kicked goal, making the score 12 to 11 in Erskine's favor. For the rest of the half the home team was satisfied to keep Woodby away from its goal, and made no effort to score. Woodby left the field after the fashion of victors, which, practically, they were, while the Erskine players trotted subduedly back to the locker-house with unpleasant anticipations of what was before them - anticipations fully justified by subsequent events. For Mills tore them up very eloquently, and promised them that if they were scored on by the second eleven before the game with Harvard he'd send every man of them to the benches and take the second to Cambridge.

Neil walked back to college beside Sydney Burr, insisting that that youth should take his hands from the levers and be pushed. Paul had got into the habit of always accompanying Cowan on his return from the field, and as Neil liked the big sophomore less and less the more he saw of him, he usually fell back on either Ted Foster or Sydney Burr for company. To-day it was Sydney. On the way that youth surprised Neil by his intelligent discussion and criticism of the game he had just watched.

"How on earth did you get to know so much about football?" asked Neil. "You talk like a varsity coach."

"Do I?" said Sydney, flushing with pleasure. "I - I always liked the game, and I've studied it quite a bit and watched it all I could. Of course, I can never play, but I get a good deal of enjoyment out of it. Sometimes" - his shyness returned momentarily and he hesitated - "sometimes I make believe that I'm playing, you know; put myself, in imagination, in the place of one of the team. To-day I - to-day I was you," he added with a deprecatory laugh.

"You don't say?" cried Neil. Then the pathos of it struck him and he was silent a moment. The cripple's love and longing for sport in which he could never hope to join seemed terribly sad and gave him a choking sensation in his throat.

"If I had been - like other fellows," continued Sydney, quite cheerfully, "I should have played everything - football, baseball, hockey, tennis - everything! I'd give - anything I've got - if I could just run from here to the corner." He was silent a minute, looking before him with eyes from which the usual brightness was gone. Then, "My, it must be good to run and walk and jump around just as you want to," he sighed.

"Yes," muttered Neil, "but - but that was a good little run you made to-day." Sydney looked puzzled, then laughed.

"In the game, you mean? Yes, wasn't it? And I made a touch-down and won the game. I was awfully afraid at one time that that Woodby quarter-back was going to nab me; that's why I made for the corner of the field like that."

"I fancied that was the reason," answered Neil gravely. Then their eyes met and they laughed together.

"Your friend Gale didn't play so well to-day," said Sydney presently. Neil shook his head with a troubled air.

"No, he played rotten ball, and that's a fact. I don't know what's got into him of late. He doesn't seem to care whether he pleases Mills or not. I think it's that chap Cowan. He tells Paul that Mills and Devoe are imposing on him and that he isn't getting a fair show and all that sort of stuff. Know Cowan?"

"Only by sight. I don't think I'd care to know him; he looks a good deal like - like -"

"Just so," laughed Neil. "That's the way he strikes me."

After dinner that evening Paul bewailed what he called his ill luck. Neil listened patiently for a while; then -

"Look here, Paul," he said, "don't talk such rot. Luck had nothing to do with it, and you know it. The trouble was that you weren't in shape; you've been shilly-shallying around of late and just doing good enough work to keep Mills from dropping you to the scrub. It's that miserable idiot Tom

Cowan that's to blame; he's been filling your head with nonsense; telling you that you are so good that you don't have to practise, and that Mills doesn't dare drop you, and lots of poppycock of that kind. Now, I'll tell you, chum, that the best thing to do is to go honestly to work and do your best."

Paul was deeply insulted by this plain speaking, and very promptly took himself off up-stairs to Cowan's room. Of late he spent a good deal of his time there and Neil was getting worried. For Cowan was notably an idler, and the wonder was how he managed to keep himself in college even though he was taking but a partial course. To be sure, Cowan's fate didn't bother Neil a bit, but he was greatly afraid that his example would be followed by his roommate, who, at the best, was none too fond of study. Neil sat long that evening over an unopened book, striving to think of some method of weakening Cowan's hold on Paul - a hold that was daily growing stronger and which threatened to work ill to the latter. In the end Neil sighed, tossed down the volume, and made ready for bed without having found a solution of the problem.

The following Monday Neil was rewarded for his good showing in the Woodby game by being taken on to the varsity. Paul remained on the second team, and Cowan, greatly to that gentleman's bewilderment and wrath, joined him there. The two teams, with their substitutes, went to training-table that day in Pearson's boarding-house on Elm Street, and preparation for the game with Harvard, now but nine days distant, began in earnest.

Ralph Henry Barbour

CHAPTER XI

THE RESULT OF A FUMBLE

Sydney Burr had trundled himself out to the field and had drawn his tricycle close up to the low wooden fence that divides the gridiron from the grand stand and against which the players on the benches lean their blanketed backs. From there he had an uninterrupted view. It was a perfect afternoon. Overhead a few white clouds drifted lazily about against a warm blue sky. The sun shone brightly and mocked at light overcoats. But for all that there was an October sparkle in the air, and once in a while a tiny breeze from the north came across the yellowing field and whispered that winter was not far behind.

Sydney had a rug thrown over his lower limbs and wore a warm white woolen sweater. There was quite a dash of color in his usually pale cheeks, and his blue eyes flashed with interest as he watched the men at practise. Near at hand a panting group of fellows were going through the signals, the quarter crying his numbers with gasps for breath, then passing the ball to half-or full-back and quickly throwing himself into the interference. Sydney recognized him as Bailey, the varsity substitute. Sydney knew almost all the players by sight now and the names of many.

Near the east goal two lines of heaving, charging men were being coached by Mills in breaking through. Stowell, the big, good-natured substitute center, was bending over the ball.

Sydney could hear Mills's sharp voice:

"Now draw back, defense, and lunge into them! Get the start on them!"

Then the ball was snapped and the two ranks heaved and pitched a moment before the offense broke through and scattered the turf with little clumps of writhing players.

"That was good, Tucker, good!" cried Mills. "You did just as I told you. Now give the ball to the other side. Weight forward, defense, every one of you on his toes. *Browning, watch that ball!* Now get into them, every one! Block them!"

At the other end of the field six fellows were kicking goal and six others, stretched upon the turf, were holding the balls for them. Devoe was coaching. Sydney could see Neil, the farthest away of any, lifting the leather toward the posts from a difficult angle on the twenty-yard line. Even as he watched, the ball sailed away from Neil's toe and went fair over the cross-bar, and Sydney silently applauded. He set himself to recognizing the other kickers. There was Gale, the tall and rather heavy fellow in the crimson sleeves; and Mason, equally tall but all corners and angles; and Smith, and Gillam, and Foster. Devoe seemed to be laying down the law forcibly to Gale; he was gesticulating with his hands and nodding his head like a Chinese mandarin. Sydney could not hear what he was saying, nor could he see Gale's face; but in the attitude of the captain there was exasperation, and in that of Gale sullen impatience.

Another group at signal practise drew nigh, and Sydney gave his attention to it. Reardon, the second eleven quarter, sang his signals in a queer, shrill voice that was irresistibly funny. In front of Sydney he raised himself, wiped his palms on his stained trousers, grimaced at one of the halves, and took a deep breath. Then -

"*Signal!*" he cried. "*7 - 8 - 4 - 6!*"

Eight half bounded by him, full-back fell in behind and took the ball, left half dashed after, and the group trotted away to line up again ten yards down the field. But presently the lines at the east goal broke up and trotted toward the benches, and Mills called the players in from all parts of the field. The water-pail was surrounded and the thirsty players rinsed out their mouths, well knowing the reprimand that awaited should they be rash enough to take even one swallow. Sweaters were hurriedly donned, Simson dealing them out from the pile on the ground, and the fellows sank on to the benches. Neil saw Sydney, and talked to him over the fence until he heard his name called from the line-up.

"I think I shall make a touch-down to-day," said Sydney. Neil shook his head, smiling:

"I don't know about that; you're not feeling so fit to-day, you know."

"Oh, that doesn't matter," answered the cripple. "You just watch me."

Neil laughed, and hurrying off, was fitted with his head harness and trotted out to his place. Sydney was mistaken, as events proved, for he - in the person of Neil Fletcher - failed to get over the second's goal-line in either of the short halves; which was also true of all the other varsity players. But if she didn't score, the varsity kept the second at bay, and that was a good deal. The second played desperately, being convinced that Mills would keep his promise and, if they succeeded in scoring on their opponents, give them the honor of facing Harvard the following Wednesday. But the varsity, being equally convinced of the fact, played quite as desperately, and the two teams trotted off with honors even.

"Sponge off, everybody!" was the stentorian command from the trainer, and one by one the players leaned over while the big, dripping sponge was applied to face and head. Then sweaters were again donned and the four laps around the field began, the men trotting by twos and threes, or, in the case of the injured ones, trailing along behind.

The next day, Wednesday, October 16th, Erskine played Dexter. Dexter is a preparatory school that has a way of turning out strong elevens, many of which in previous years had put up excellent fights against Erskine. On the present occasion Erskine went into the game with a line largely composed of substitutes and a back-field by no means as strong as possible. During the first half Dexter was forced to give all her attention to defending her goal, and had no time for incursions into Erskine territory. The home college ran up 17 points, Devoe missing one goal. In the second half Erskine made further changes in her team. Cowan took Witter's place at right-guard, Reardon went in at quarter in place of Bailey, and Neil, who had watched the first half greedily from the side-line, went in at left half.

It was Dexter's kick-off, and she sent the ball fully forty yards. Reardon called to Neil to take it. That youth got it on his ten yards, and by fine dodging ran it back to the eighteen-yard line. From there it was advanced by straight line-plunging to Erskine's forty yards, and it seemed that a procession down the field to another touch-down had begun. But at this point Fate and Tom Cowan took a hand. Cowan was taken back of the line for a plunge through tackle. With right half and full lined up in tandem behind him he was given the ball and shot through easily for several yards. Then, his support gone, he staggered on for five yards more by sheer force of weight with two Dexter backs dragging at him, and there, for no apparent cause, dropped the pigskin. The Dexter quarter-back, running in to stop Cowan, was on it in a twinkling, had skirted the right end of the *melee* and was racing toward Erskine's goal. sIt had happened so quickly and unexpectedly that the runner was fifteen yards to the good before pursuit began. Devoe and Neil took up the chase, but it was a hopeless task, and in another minute the little band of crimson-adorned Dexter supporters and substitutes on the side-line were yelling like mad. The Dexter quarter placed the ball nicely behind the very

Ralph Henry Barbour

center of the west goal, and when it was taken out none but a cripple could have failed to kick it over the cross-bar. As Dexter's left-end was not a cripple her score changed from a 5 to a 6.

But that was the end of her offensive work for that afternoon. Erskine promptly took the ball from her after the kick-off, and kept it until Neil had punctured Dexter's line between left-guard and tackle and waded through a sea of clutching foes twelve yards for a touch-down. Devoe once more failed at goal, and five minutes later the game came to an end with the final score 22 to 6. Dexter was happy and Erskine disgruntled.

In the locker-house after the game Mills had some sharp things to say, and didn't hesitate to say them in his best manner. There was absolutely no favoritism shown; he began at one end of the line and went to the other, then dropped back to left half, took in quarter on the way, and ended up with full. Some got off easy; Neil was among them; and so was Devoe, for it is not a good policy for a coach to endanger a captain's authority by public criticism; but when it was all over no one felt slighted. And when all were beginning to breathe easier, thinking the storm had passed, it burst forth anew.

"Cowan, I don't see how you came to drop that ball," said Mills, in fresh exasperation. "Why, great Scott, man, there was no one touching you except a couple of schoolboys tugging at your legs! What was the matter? Paralysis? Vertigo? Or haven't you learned yet, after two years of football playing, to hang on to the ball? There's a cozy nook waiting on the second scrub for fellows like you!"

Cowan, his pride already sorely wounded, found the last too much for his temper.

"No one can help an occasional accident," he blurted. "If I did fumble, there's no reason why you should insult me. Lots of fellows have fumbled before and got off without being walked on. I've played my position for two years, and I guess I know how to do it. But when a fellow is singled out as a - a scape-goat -"

"That will do, Cowan," interrupted Mills quietly. "You've lost your temper. We don't want men on this team who can't stand criticism -"

"Criticism!" sneered Cowan, looking very red and ugly.

"Yes, criticism!" answered Mills sharply, "and scolding, too, my friend. I'm here to turn out a team that will win from Robinson and not to cater to any one's vanity; when it's necessary, I'm going to scold and say some hard things. But I've never insulted any fellow and I never will. I've had my eye on you ever since practise began, Cowan, and let me tell you that you haven't at any time passed muster; your playing's been slovenly, careless, and generally mean. You've soldiered half the time. And I think we can get along without you for the rest of the season."

Mills, his blue eyes sparkling, turned away, and Stowell and White, who for a minute past had been striving to check Cowan's utterances, now managed to drag him away.

"Shut up!" whispered White hoarsely. "Don't be a fool! Come out of here!" And they hauled him outside, where, on the porch, he gave vent anew to his wrath until they left him finally in disgust.

He slouched in to see Paul after dinner that evening, much to Neil's impatience, and taking up a commanding position on a corner of the study-table, recited his tale of injustice with great eloquence. Paul, who had spent the afternoon with other unfortunates on the benches, was full of sympathy.

"It's a dirty shame, Tom," he said. "And I'm glad you waded into Mills the way you did. It was fine!"

"Little white-haired snake!" exclaimed Cowan. "Drops me

from training just because I make a fumble! Why, you've fumbled, Paul, and so's Fletcher here; lots of times. But he doesn't lay *you* off! Oh, dear, no; you're swells whose names will look well in the line-up for the Robinson game! But here I've played on the team for two years, and now off I go just because I dropped a ball. It's rank injustice!

"I suppose he thinks I've got to play football here. If he does he's away off, that's all. I could have gone to Robinson this fall and had everything I wanted. They guaranteed me a position at guard or tackle, and I wouldn't have needed to bother with studies as I do here, either." The last remark called a smile to Neil's face, and Cowan unfortunately glanced his way and saw it.

"I dare say if I was willing to toady to Mills and Devoe, and tell everybody they're the finest football leaders that ever came down the pike, it would be different," he sneered angrily. "Maybe then Mills would give me private instruction in goal-kicking and let me black his boots for him."

Neil closed his book and leaned back in his chair, a little disk of red in each cheek.

"Now, look here, Tom Cowan, let's have this out," he said quietly. "You're hitting at me, of course -"

"Oh, keep out, chum," protested Paul. "Cowan hasn't mentioned you once."

"He doesn't need to," answered Neil. "I understand without it. But let me tell you, Cowan, that I do not toady to either Mills or Devoe. I do treat them, however, as I would any one who was in authority over me. I don't think merely because I've played the game before that I know all the football there is to know."

"Meaning that I do?" growled Cowan.

"I mean that you've got a swelled head, Cowan, and that when Mills said you hadn't been doing your best he only told the truth, and what every fellow knows."

"Shut up, Neil!" cried Paul angrily. "It isn't necessary for you to pitch into Cowan just because he's down on his luck."

"I don't mind him," said Cowan, eying Neil with hatred. "He's sore about what I said. I dare say I shouldn't have said it. If he's Mills's darling -"

Neil pushed back his chair, and rose to his feet with blazing eyes.

"Kindly get out of here," he said. "I've had enough of your insults. This is my room; please leave it!" Cowan stared a moment in surprise, hesitated, threw a glance of inquiry at Paul's troubled and averted face, and slid from the table.

"Of course you can put me out of your room," he sneered. "For that matter, I'm glad to leave it. I did think, though, that part of the shop was Paul's, but I dare say he has to humor you."

"The room's as much mine as his," said Paul, "and I want you to stay in it." He looked defiantly over at his friend. Neil had not bargained for a quarrel with Paul, but was too incensed to back down.

"And I say you sha'n't stay," he declared. "Paul and I will settle the proprietorship of the room after you're out of it. Now you get!"

"Maybe you'll put me out?" asked Cowan with a show of bravado. But he glanced toward the door as he spoke. Neil nodded.

"Maybe I will," he answered grimly.

"Cowan's my guest, Neil!" cried Paul. "And you've no right to put him out, and I sha'n't let you!"

"He'll go out of here, if I have to fight him and you too, Paul!" Paul stared in wonderment. He was so used to being humored by his roommate that this declaration of war took his breath away. Cowan laughed with attempted nonchalance.

"Your friend's a bit chesty, Paul," he said. "Perhaps we'd better humor him."

"No, stay where you are," said Paul. "If he thinks he's boss of me he's mistaken." He glared wrathfully at Neil, and yet with a trifle of uneasiness. Paul was no coward, but physical conflict with Neil was something so contrary to the natural order that it appalled him. Neil removed the gorgeous bottle-green velvet jacket that he wore in the evenings, and threw open the study door. Then he faced Cowan. That gentleman returned his gaze for a moment defiantly. But something in Neil's expression caused his eyes to drop and seek the portal. He laughed uneasily, and with simulated indifference laid his hand on Paul's shoulder.

"Come on, old chap," he said, "let's get out before we're torn to bits. There's no pleasure in staying with such a disagreeable fire-eater, anyhow. Come up to my room, and let him cool off."

Paul hesitated, and then turned to follow Cowan, who was strolling toward the door. Angry as he was, deep in his heart he was glad to avoid conflict with his chum.

"All right," he answered in a voice that trembled, "we'll go; but" - turning to Neil - "if you think I'm going to put up with this sort of thing, you're mistaken. You can have this room, and I'll get another."

"I'd suggest your rooming with Cowan," answered Neil, "since you're so fond of him."

"Your friend's jealous," laughed Cowan from the hall. Paul joined him, slamming the door loudly as he went.

Neil heard Cowan's laughter and the sound of their steps as they climbed the stairs. For several moments he stood motionless, staring at the door. Then he shook his head, donned his jacket, and sat down again. Now that it was done, he was intensely sorry. As for the quarrel with Cowan, that troubled not at all; but an open breach with Paul was something new and something which, just at this time especially, might work for ill. Paul was already so far under Cowan's domination that anything tending to foster their friendship was unfortunate. Neil was ashamed, too, of his burst of temper, and the remainder of the evening passed miserably enough.

When Paul returned he was cold and repellent, and answered Neil's attempts at conversation in monosyllables. Neil, however, was glad to find that Paul said nothing further about a change of quarters, and in that fact found encouragement. After all, Paul would soon get over his anger, he told himself; the two had been firm friends for three years, and it would take something more than the present affair to estrange them.

But as the days passed and Paul showed no disposition to make friends again, Neil began to despair. He knew that Cowan was doing all in his power to widen the breach and felt certain that left to himself Paul would have forgotten his grievance long ago. Paul spent most of his time in Cowan's room when at home, and Neil passed many dull hours. One thing there was, however, which pleased him. Cowan's absence from the field worked a difference from the first in Paul's playing, and the latter was now evidently putting his heart into his work. He made such a good showing between the day of Cowan's dismissal and the following Wednesday that he was scheduled to play right half against Harvard, and was consequently among the little army of players and supporters that journeyed to Cambridge on that day.

CHAPTER XII

ON THE HOSPITAL LIST

Harvard's good showing thus far during the season convinced Erskine that could she hold the crimson warriors down to five scores she would be doing remarkably well, and that could she, by any miracle, cross Harvard's goal-line she would be practically victorious. The team that journeyed to Cambridge on October 23d was made up as follows:

Stone, l.e.; Tucker, l.t.; Carey, l.g.; Stowell, c.; Witter, r.g.; White, r.t.; Devoe, r.e.; Foster, q.b.; Fletcher, l.h.b.; Gale, r.h.b.; Mason, f.b.

Besides these, eight substitutes went along and some thirty patriotic students followed. Among the latter was Sydney Burr and "Fan" Livingston. Neil had brought the two together, and Livingston had readily taken to the crippled youth. In Livingston's care Sydney had no difficulty in making the trip to Soldiers Field and back comfortably and safely.

There is no need to tell in detail here of the Harvard-Erskine contest. Those who saw it will give Erskine credit for a plucky struggle against a heavier, more advanced, and much superior team. In the first half Harvard scored three times, and the figures were 17-0. In the second half both teams put in several substitutes. For Erskine, Browning went in for Carey, Graham for Stowell, Hurst for Witter, Pearse for Mason, and Bailey for Foster. In this half Harvard crossed Erskine's goal-line three more times without much difficulty, while Erskine made the most of a stroke of rare good luck, and changed her goose-egg for the figure 5.

On the Purple's forty yards Harvard fumbled, not for the first time that day, and Neil, more by accident than design, got the pigskin on the bounce, and, skirting the opposing right end, went up the field for a touch down without ever being in danger. The Erskine supporters went mad with delight, and the Harvard stand was ruefully silent. Devoe missed a difficult goal and a few minutes later the game ended with a final score of 34-5. Mills, however, would gladly have yielded that five points, if by so doing he could have taken ten from the larger score. He was disappointed in the team's defense, and realized that a wonderful improvement was necessary if Robinson was to be defeated.

And so the Erskine players were plainly given to understand the next day that they had not acquired all the glory they thought they had. The advance guard of the assistant coaches put in an appearance in the shape of Jones and Preston, both old Erskine football men, and took hold with a vim. Jones, a former guard, a big man with bristling black hair, took the line men under his wing and made them jump. Neil, Paul, and several others were taken in hand by Preston, and were daily put through a vigorous course of punting and kicking. Neil was fast acquiring speed and certainty in the art of kicking goals from drop and placement, while Paul promised to turn out a fair second choice.

Jones, as every one soon learned, was far from satisfied with the line of material at his disposal. He wanted more weight, especially in the center trio, and was soon pleading with Mills to have Cowan reinstated. The head coach ultimately relented, and Devoe was given to understand that if Cowan expressed himself decently regretful and determined to do good work he could go back into the second. The big sophomore, who, by his frequent avowals, was in college for no other purpose than to play football, had simply been lost since his dismissal, and, upon hearing Devoe's message, eagerly came off his high horse and made a visit to Mills. What he said and what Mills said is not known; but Cowan went back into the second team at right-guard, and on Saturday was given a try at that position in the game with Erstham. He did so well that Jones was highly pleased, and Mills found it in his heart to forgive. The results of the Erstham game were both unexpected and important.

Instead of the comparatively easy victory anticipated, Erskine barely managed to save herself from being played to a standstill, and the final figures were 6-0 in her favor. The score was made in the last eight minutes of the second half by fierce line-bucking, but not before half of the purple line had given place to substitutes, and one of the back-field had been carried bodily off the gridiron.

With the ball on Erstham's twenty-six yards, where it had been desperately carried by the relentless plunging and hurdling of Neil, Smith, and Mason, Erstham twice successfully repelled the onslaught, and it was Erskine's third down with two yards to gain. To lose the ball by kicking was the last thing to be thought of, and so, despite the fact that hitherto well-nigh every attempt at end running had met with failure, Foster gave the ball to Neil for a try around the Erstham left end. It was a forlorn hope, and unfortunately Erstham was looking for it. Neil found his outlet blocked by his own interference, and was forced to run far out into the field. The play was a failure from the first. Erstham's big right half and an equally big line man tackled Neil simultaneously for a loss and threw him heavily.

When they got off him Neil tried to arise, but, with a groan, subsided again on the turf. The whistle blew and Simson ran on. Neil was evidently suffering a good deal of pain, for his face was ashen and he rolled his head from side to side with eyes half closed. His right arm lay outstretched and without movement, and in an instant the trouble was found. Simson examined the injury quickly and called for the doctor, who probed Neil's shoulder with knowing fingers, while the latter's white face was being sopped with the dripping sponge.

"Right shoulder's dislocated, Jim," said Dr. Prentiss quietly to the trainer. "Take hold here; put your hands here, and pull toward you steadily. Now!"

Then Neil fainted.

When he regained consciousness he was being borne from the field between four of his fellows. At the locker-house the injured shoulder was laid bare, and the doctor went to work.

The pain had subsided, and only a queer soreness remained. Neil watched operations with interest, his face fast regaining its color.

"Nothing much, is it?" he asked.

"Not a great deal. You've smashed your shoulder-blade a bit, and maybe torn a ligament. I'll fix you up in a minute."

"Will it keep me from playing?"

"Yes, for a while, my boy."

Bandage after bandage was swathed about the shoulder, and the arm was fixed in what Neil conceived to be the most unnatural and awkward position possible.

"How long is this going to lay me up?" he asked anxiously. But the doctor shook his head.

"Can't tell yet. We'll see how you get along."

"Well, a week?"

"Maybe."

"Two?"

"Possibly."

"But - but it can't! It mustn't!" he cried. The door opened and Simson entered. "Simson," he called, "he says this may keep me laid up for two weeks. It won't, will it?"

"I hope not, Fletcher. But you must get it well healed, or else it may go back on you again. Don't worry about -"

"Don't worry! But, great Scott, the Robinson game's only a month off!"

The trainer patted his arm soothingly.

"I know, but we must make the best of it. It's hard lines, but the only thing to do is to take care of yourself and get well as soon as possible. The doc will get you out again as soon as it can be done, but you'll have to be doing your part, Fletcher, and keeping quiet and cheerful -"

"Cheerful!" groaned Neil.

"And getting strong. Now you're fixed and I'll go over to your room with you. How do you feel?"

"All right, I suppose," replied Neil hopelessly.

Simson walked beside him back to college and across the campus and the common to his room, and saw him installed in an easy-chair with a pillow behind the injured shoulder.

"There you are," said the trainer. "Prentiss will look in this evening and I'll see you in the morning. You'd better keep indoors for a few days, you know. I'll have your meals sent over. Don't worry about this, but keep yourself cheerful and -"

Neil leaned his head against the pillow and closed his eyes.

"Oh, go 'way," he muttered miserably.

When Paul came in half an hour later he found Neil staring

motionless out of the window, settled melancholy on his face.

"How bad is it, chum?" asked Paul. He hadn't called Neil "chum" for over a week - not since their quarrel.

"Bad enough to spoil my chances for the Robinson game," answered Neil bitterly. Paul gave vent to a low whistle.

"By Jove! I am sorry, old chap. That's beastly, isn't it? What does Prentiss say?"

Neil told him and gained some degree of animation in fervid protestation against his fate. For want of another, he held the doctor to account for everything, only admitting Simson to an occasional share in the blame. Paul looked genuinely distressed, joining him in denunciation of Prentiss and uttering such bits of consolation as occurred to him. These generally consisted of such original remarks as "Perhaps it won't be as bad as they think." "I don't believe doctors know everything, after all." "Mills will make them get you around before two weeks, I'll bet."

After dinner Paul returned to report a state of general gloom at training-table.

"Every one's awfully sorry and cut up about it, chum. Mills says he'll come and look you up in the morning, and told me to tell you to keep your courage up." After his information had given out, Paul walked restlessly about the study, taking up book after book only to lay it down again, and behaving generally like a fish out of water. Neil, grateful for the other's sympathy, and secretly delighted at the healing of the breach, could afford to be generous.

"I say, Paul, I'll be all right. Just give me the immortal Livy, will you? Thanks. And you might put that tray out of the way somewhere and shove the drop-light a bit nearer. That's better. I'll be all right now; you run along."

"Run along where?" asked Paul.

"Well, I thought maybe you were going out or - somewhere."

Paul's face expressed astonishment. He took up a book and settled himself firmly in the wicker rocking-chair.

"No," he said, "I'm not going anywhere."

Neil studied in silence a while, and Paul turned several pages of his book. Then footsteps sounded on the stairs and Cowan's voice hailed Paul from beyond the closed door.

"O Paul, are you coming along?"

Paul glanced irresolutely from the door to Neil's face, which was bent calmly over his book. Then - "No," he called gruffly, "not to-night!"

CHAPTER XIII

SYDNEY STUDIES STRATEGY

Neil was holding a levee. Livingston shared the couch with him. Foster reclined in Paul's armchair. Sydney Burr sat in the protesting wicker rocker, his crutches beside him, and South, his countenance much disfigured by strips of surgeon's plaster, grinned steadily from the table, where he sat and swung his feet. Paul was up-stairs in Cowan's room, for while he and Neil had quite made up their difference, and while Paul spent much of his leisure time with his chum, yet he still cultivated the society of the big sophomore at intervals. Neil, however, believed he could discern a gradual lessening of Paul's regard for Cowan, and was encouraged. He had grown to look upon his injury and the idleness it enforced with some degree of cheerfulness since it had brought about reconciliation between him and his roommate, and, as he believed, rescued the latter to some extent from the influence of Cowan.

"Doc says the shoulder is 'doing nicely,' whatever that may mean," Neil was saying, "and that I will likely be able to get back to light work next week." The announcement didn't sound very joyful, for it was now only the evening of the fourth day since the accident, and "next week" seemed a long way off to him.

"It was hard luck, old man," said South.

"Your sympathy's very dear to me," answered Neil, "but it

would seem more genuine if you'd stop grinning from ear to ear."

"Can't," replied South. "It's the plaster."

"He's been looking like the Cheshire cat for two days," said Livingston. "You see, when they patched him up they asked if he was suffering much agony, and he grinned that way just to show that he was a hero, and before he could get his face straight they had the plaster on. He gets credit for being much better natured than he really is."

"Credit!" said South. "I get worse than that. 'Sandy' saw me grinning at him in class yesterday and got as mad as a March hare; said I was 'deesrespectful.'"

"But how did it happen?" asked Neil, struggling with his laughter.

"Lacrosse," replied South. "Murdoch was tending goal and I was trying to get the ball by him. I tripped over his stick and banged my face against a goal-iron. That's all."

"Seems to me it's enough," said Foster. "What did you do to Murdoch?" South opened his eyes in innocent surprise.

"Nothing."

"Nothing be blowed, my boy. Murdoch's limping to beat the band."

"Oh!" grinned South. "That was afterward; he got mixed up with my stick, and, I fear, hurt his shins."

"Well," said Neil, when the laughter was over, "football seems deadly enough, but I begin to think it's a parlor game for rainy evenings alongside of lacrosse."

"There won't be many fellows left for the Robinson game,"

said Sydney, "if they keep on getting hurt."

"That's so," Livingston concurred. "Fletcher, White, Jewell, Brown, Stowell - who else?"

"Well, I'm not feeling well myself," said Foster.

"We were referring to *players*, Teddy, my love," replied South sweetly.

"Insulted!" cried Foster, leaping wildly to his feet. "It serves me right for associating with a lot of freshmen. Good-night, Fletcher, my wounded gladiator. Get well and come back to us; all will be forgiven."

"I'd like the chance of forgiving the fellow that jumped on my shoulder," said Neil. "I'd send him to join Murdoch."

"That's not nice," answered Foster gravely. "Forgive your enemies. Good-night, you cubs."

"Hold on," said Livingston, "I'm going your way. Good-night, Fletcher. Cheer up and get well. We need you and so does the team. Remember the class is looking forward to seeing you win a few touch-downs in the Robinson game."

"Oh, I'll be all right," answered Neil, "and if they'll let me into the game I'll do my best. Only - I'm afraid I'll be a bit stale when I get out again."

"Not you," declared Livingston heartily. "'Age can not wither nor custom stale your infinite variety.'"

"That's a quotation from - somebody," said South accusingly. "'Fan' wants us to think he made it up. Besides, I don't think it's correct; it should be, 'Custom can not age nor wither stale your various interests.' Hold on, I'm not particular; I'll walk along with you two. But fortune send we don't meet the Dean," he continued, as he slid to the floor. "I called on him

Monday; a little affair of too many cuts; 'Mr. South,' said he sorrowfully, 'avoid two things while in college - idleness and evil associations.' I promised, fellows, and here I am breaking that promise. Farewell, Fletcher; bear up under your great load of affliction. Good-night, Burr. Kindly see that he gets his medicine regularly every seven minutes, and don't let him sleep in a draft; pajamas are much warmer."

"Come on, you grinning idiot," said Foster.

When the door had closed upon the three, Sydney placed his crutches under his arms and moved over to the chair beside the couch.

"Look here, Neil, you don't really think, do you, that you'll have any trouble getting back into your place?"

"I hardly know. Of course two weeks of idleness makes a big difference. And besides, I'm losing a lot of practise. This new close-formation that Mills is teaching will be Greek to me."

"It's simple enough," said Sydney. "The backs are bunched right up to the line, the halfs on each side of quarter, and the full just behind him."

"Well, but I don't see -"

"Wait," interrupted Sydney, "I'll show you."

He drew a folded sheet of paper from his pocket and passed it to the other. Neil scowled over it a moment, and then looked up helplessly.

"What is it?" he asked. "Something weird in geometry?"

"No," laughed Sydney, "it's a play from close-formation. I drew it this morning."

"Oh," said Neil. "Let's see; what - Here, explain it; where do I come in?"

"Why, your position is at the left of quarter, behind the center-guard, and a little farther back. Full stands directly behind quarter. See?"

"Pshaw! if we get into a crowd like that," said Neil, "we'll get all tied up."

"No you won't; not the way Mills and Devoe are teaching it. You see, the idea is to knife the backs through; there isn't any plunging to speak of and not much hurdling. The forwards open up a hole, and almost before the ball's well in play one of the backs is squirming through. Quarter gives you the ball at a hand-pass, always; there's no long passing done; except, of course, for a kick. Being right up to the line when play begins it only takes you a fraction of a second to hit it; and then, if the hole's there you're through before the other side has opened their eyes. Of course, it all depends on speed and the ability of the line-men to make holes. You've got to be on your toes, and you've got to get off them like a streak of lightning."

"Well, maybe it's all right," said Neil doubtfully, "but it looks like a mix-up. Who gets the ball in this play here?"

"Right half. Left half plunges through between left-guard and center to make a diversion. Full-back goes through between left tackle and end ahead of right half, who carries the ball. Quarter follows. Of course the play can be made around end instead. What do you think of it?"

"All right; but - I think I'd ought to have the ball."

"You would when the play went to the right," laughed Sydney. "The fact is, I - this particular play hasn't been used. I sort of got it up myself. I don't know whether it would be any good. I sometimes try my hand at inventing plays, just for fun, you know."

"Really?" exclaimed Neil. "Well, you are smart. I could no more draw all those nice little cakes and pies and things than I could fly. And it - it looks plausible, I think. But I'm no authority on this sort of thing. Are you going to show it to Devoe?"

"Oh, no; I dare say it's no use. It may be as old as the hills; I suppose it is. It's hard to find anything new nowadays in football plays."

"But you don't know," said Neil. "Maybe it's a good thing. I'll tell you, Syd, you let me have this, and I'll show it to Mills."

"Oh, I'd rather not," protested Sydney, reddening. "Of course it doesn't amount to anything; I dare say he's thought of it long ago."

"But maybe he hasn't," Neil persuaded. "Come, let me show it to him, like a good chap."

"Well - But couldn't you let him think you did it?"

"No; I'd be up a tree if he asked me to explain it. But don't you be afraid of Mills; he's a fine chap. Come and see me to-morrow night, will you?"

Sydney agreed, and, arising, swung himself across the study to where his coat and cap lay.

"By the way," he asked, "where's Paul to-night?"

"He's calling on Cowan," answered Neil.

Sydney looked as though he wanted to say something and didn't dare. Finally he found courage.

"I should think he'd stay in his room now that you're laid up," he said.

"Oh, he does," answered Neil. "Paul's all right, only he's a bit - careless. I guess I've humored him too much. Good-night. Don't forget to-morrow night."

Mills called the following forenoon. Ever since Neil's accident he had made it his duty to inquire daily after him, and the two were getting very well acquainted. Neil likened Mills to a crab - rather crusty on the outside, he told himself, but all right when you got under the shell. Neil was getting under the shell.

To-day, after Neil had reported on his state of health and spirits, he brought out Sydney's diagram. Mills examined it carefully, silently, for some time. Then he nodded his head.

"Not bad; rather clever. Who did it; you?"

"No, I couldn't if I was to be killed. Sydney Burr did it. Maybe you've seen him. A cripple; goes around on a tricycle."

"Yes, I've seen the boy. But does he - has he played?"

"Never; he's been a crip all his life." Mills opened his eyes in astonishment.

"Well, if that's so this is rather wonderful. It's a good play, Fletcher, but it's not original; that is, not altogether. But as far as Burr's concerned it is, of course. Look here, the fellow ought to be encouraged. I'll see him and tell him to try his hand again."

"He's coming here this evening," said Neil. "Perhaps you could look in for a moment?"

"I will. Let me take this; I want Jones to see it. He thinks he's a wonder at diagrams," laughed Mills, "and I want to tell him this was got up by a crippled freshman who has never kicked a ball!"

And so that evening Mills and Neil and Sydney gathered about the big study-table and talked long about gridiron tactics and strategy and the art of inventing plays. Mills praised Sydney's production and encouraged him to try again.

"But let me tell you first how we're situated," said the head coach, "so that you will see just what we're after. Our material is good but light. Robinson will come into the field on the twenty-third weighing about eight pounds more to a man in the line and ten pounds more behind it. That's bad enough, but she's going to play tackle-back about the way we've taught the second eleven to play it. Her tackles will weigh about one hundred and eighty-five pounds each. She will take one of those men, range him up in front of our center-guard hole, and put two backs with him, tandem fashion. When that trio, joined by the other half and the quarter, hits our line it's going right through it - that is, unless we can find some means of stopping it. So far we haven't found that means. We've tried several things; we're still trying; but we haven't found the play we want.

"If we're to win that game we've got to play on the defensive; we've got to stop tackle-back and rely on an end run now and then and lots of punting to get us within goal distance. Then our play is to score by a quick run or a field-goal. The offense we're working up - we'll call it close-formation for want of a better name - is, we think, the best we can find. The idea is to open holes quickly and jab a runner through before our heavier and necessarily slower opponents can concentrate their weight at the point of attack. For the close-formation we have, I think, plays covering every phase. And so, while a good offensive strategy will be welcome, yet what we stand in greatest need of is a play to stop Robinson's tackle-tandem. Now you apparently have ability in this line, Mr. Burr; and, what's more, you have the time to study the thing up. Supposing you try your hand and see what you can do. If you can find what we want - something that the rest of us can't find, by the way - you'll be doing as much, if not more, than any of us toward securing a victory over Robinson. And don't hesitate to come and see me if you find yourself in a quandary or whenever you've got anything to show."

And Sydney trundled himself back to his room and sat up until after midnight puzzling his brains over the tackle-tandem play, finally deciding that a better understanding of the play was necessary before he could hope to discover its remedy. When he crawled into bed and closed his tired eyes it was to see a confused jumble of orange-hued lines and circles running riot in the darkness.

CHAPTER XIV

MAKES A CALL

Despite Neil's absence from Erskine Field, preparation for the crowning conflict of the year went on with vigor and enthusiasm. The ranks of the coaches were swelled from day to day by patriotic alumni, some of whom were of real help, others of whom merely stood around in what Devoe called their "store clothes" and looked wonderfully wise. Some came to stay and took up quarters in the village, but the most merely tarried overnight, and, having unburdened themselves to Mills and Devoe of much advice, went away again, well pleased with their devotion to alma mater.

The signals in use during the preliminary season had now been discarded in favor of the more complicated system prepared for the "big game." Each day there was half an hour of secret practise behind closed gates, after which the assistant coaches emerged looking very wise and very solemn. The make-up of the varsity eleven had changed not a little since the game with Woodby, and was still being changed. Some positions were, however, permanently filled. For instance, Browning had firmly established his right to play left-guard, while the deposed Carey found a role eminently suited to him at right tackle. Stowell became first choice for center, and the veteran Graham went over to the second team. Stone at left end, Tucker at left tackle, Devoe at right end, and Foster at quarter, were fixtures.

The problem of finding a man for the position of left half in place of Neil had finally been solved by moving Paul over there from the other side and giving his place to Gillam, a last year substitute. Paul's style of play was very similar to Neil's. He was sure on his feet, a hard, fast runner, and his line-plunging was often brilliant and effective. The chief fault with him was that he was erratic. One day he played finely, the next so listlessly as to cause the coaches to shake their heads. His goal-kicking left something to be desired, but as yet he was as good in that line as any save Neil. Gillam, although light, was a hard line-bucker and a hurdler that was afraid of nothing. In fact he gave every indication of excelling Paul by the time the Robinson game arrived.

One cause of Paul's uneven playing was the fact that he was worried about his studies. He was taking only the required courses, seven in all, making necessary an attendance of sixteen hours each week; but Greek and mathematics were stumbling-blocks, and he was in daily fear lest he find himself forbidden to play football. He knew well enough where the trouble lay; he simply didn't give enough time to study. But, somehow, what with the all-absorbing subject of making the varsity and the hundred and one things that took up his time, the hours remaining for "grinding" were all too few. He wondered how Neil, who seemed quite as busy as himself, managed to give so much time to books.

In one of his weekly evening talks to the football men Mills had strongly counseled attention to study. There was no excuse, he had asserted, for any of the candidates shirking lessons.

"On the contrary, the fact that you are in training, that you are living with proper regard for sleep, good food, fresh air, and plenty of hard physical work, should and does make you able to study better. In my experience, I am glad to say, I have known not one football captain who did not stand among the first few in his class; and that same experience has proved to me that, almost without exception, students who go in for athletics are the best scholars. Healthful exercise and sensible living go hand in hand with scholarly attainment. I don't mean to say that every successful student has been an athlete, but I do say that almost every athlete has been a successful student. And now that we understand each other in this matter, none of you need feel any surprise if, should you get into difficulties with the faculty over your studies, I refuse, as I shall, to intercede in your behalf. I want men to deal with who are honest, hard-working athletes, and honest, hard-working students. My own experience and that of other coaches with whom I have talked, proves that the brilliant football player or crew man who sacrifices class standing for his athletic work may do for a while, but in the end is a losing investment."

And on top of that warning Paul had received one afternoon a printed postal card, filled in here and there with the pen, which was as follows:

"Erskine College, *November 4, 1901.*

"Mr. Paul Gale.

"Dear Sir: You are requested to call on the Dean, Tuesday, November 5th, during the regular office hours.

"Yours respectfully,

"Ephraim Levett, *Dean.*"

Paul obeyed the mandate with sinking heart. When he left the office it was with a sensation of intense relief and with a resolve to apply himself so well to his studies as to keep himself and the Dean thereafter on the merest bowing acquaintance. And he was, thus far, living up to his resolution; but as less than a week had gone by, perhaps his self-gratulation was a trifle early. It may be that Cowan also was forced to confer with the Dean at about that time, for he too showed an unusual application to text-books, and as a result he and Paul saw each other less frequently.

On November 6th, one week after Neil's accident and just two weeks prior to the Robinson game, Erskine played Arrowden, and defeated her 11-0. Neil, however, did not witness that contest, for, at the invitation of and in company with Devoe, he journeyed to Collegetown and watched Robinson play Artmouth. Devoe had rather a bad knee, and was nursing it against the game with Yale at New Haven the following Saturday. Two of the coaches were also of the party, and all were eager to get an inkling of the plays that Robinson was going to spring on Erskine. But Robinson was reticent. Perhaps her coaches discovered the presence of the Erskine emissaries. However that may have been, her team used ordinary formations instead of tackle-back, and displayed none of the tricks which rumor credited her with having up her sleeve. But the Erskine party saw enough, nevertheless, to persuade them one and all that the Purple need only expect defeat, unless some way of breaking up the tackle-back play was speedily discovered. Robinson's line was heavy, and composed almost altogether of last year material. Artmouth found it well-nigh impregnable, and Artmouth's backs were reckoned good men.

"If we had three more men in our line as heavy and steady as Browning, Cowan, and Carey," said Devoe, "we might hope to get our backs through; but, as it is, they'll get the jump on us, I fear, and tear up our offense before it gets agoing."

"The only course," answered one of the coaches, "is to get to work and put starch into the line as well as we can, and to perfect the backs at kicking and running. Luckily that close-formation has the merit of concealing the point of attack until it's under way, and it's just possible that we'll manage to fool them."

And so Jones and Mills went to work with renewed vigor the next day. But the second team, playing tackle-back after the style of Robinson's warriors, was too much for any defense that the varsity could put up, and got its distance time after time. The coaches evolved and tried several plays designed to stop it, but none proved really successful.

Neil returned to practise that afternoon, his right shoulder protected by a wonderful leather contrivance which was the cause of much good-natured fun. He didn't get near the line-up, however, but was allowed to take part in signal practise, and was then set to kicking goals from placement. If the reader will button his right arm inside his coat and try to kick a ball with accuracy he will gain some slight idea of the difficulty which embarrassed Neil. When work was over he felt as though he had been trying, he declared, to kick left-handed. But he met with enough success to demonstrate that, given opportunity for practise, one may eventually learn to kick goals minus anything except feet.

That happened to be one of Paul's "off days," and the way he played exasperated the coaches and alarmed him. He could not hide from himself the evident fact that Gillam was outplaying him five days a week. With the return of Neil, Paul expected to be ousted from the position of left half, and the question that worried him was whether he would in turn displace Gillam or be sent back to the second eleven. He was safe, however, for several days more, for Simson still laughed at Neil's demand to be put into the line-up, and he was determined that before the Yale game he would prove himself superior to Gillam.

The following morning, Friday, Mills was seated at the desk in his room making out a list of players who were to participate in the Robinson game. According to the agreement between the rival colleges such lists were required to be exchanged not later than two weeks prior to the contest. The players had been decided upon the evening before by all the coaches in assembly, and his task this morning was merely to recopy the list before him. He had almost completed the work when he heard strange sounds outside his door. Then followed a knock, and, in obedience to his request, Sydney Burr pushed open the door and swung himself in on his crutches.

The boy's face was alight with eagerness, and his eyes sparkled with excitement; there was even a dash of color in his usually pale cheeks. Mills jumped up and wheeled forward an easy-chair. But Sydney paid no heed to it.

"Mr. Mills," he cried exultantly, "I think I've got it!"

"Got what?" asked the coach.

"The play we want," answered Sydney, "the play that'll stop Robinson!"

Ralph Henry Barbour

CHAPTER XV

AND TELLS OF A DREAM

Mills's face lighted up, and he stretched forth an eager hand.

"Good for you, Burr! Let's see it. Hold on, though; sit down here first and give me those sticks. There we are. Now fire ahead."

"If you don't mind, I'd like to tell you all about it first, before I show you the diagram," said Sydney, his eyes dancing.

"All right; let's hear it," replied the head coach smiling.

"Well," began Sydney, "it's been a puzzler. After I'd seen the second playing tackle-back I about gave up hopes of ever finding a - an antidote."

"'Antidote's' good," commented Mills laughingly.

"I tried all sorts of notions," continued Sydney, "and spoiled whole reams of paper drawing diagrams. But it was all nonsense. I had the right idea, though, all the time; I realized that if that tandem was going to be stopped it would have to be stopped before it hit our line."

Mills nodded.

"I had the idea, as I say, but I couldn't apply it. And that's the way things stood last night when I went to bed. I had sat up until after eleven and had used up all the paper I had, and so when I got into bed I saw diagrams all over the place and had an awful time to get to sleep. But at last I did. And then I dreamed.

"And in the dream I was playing football. That's the first time I ever played it, and I guess it'll be the last. I was all done up in sweaters and things until I couldn't do much more than move my arms and head. It seemed that we were in 9 Grace Hall, only there was grass instead of floor, and it was all marked out like a gridiron. And everybody was there, I guess; the President and the Dean, and you and Mr. Jones, and Mr. Preston and - and my mother. It was awfully funny about my mother. She kept sewing more sweaters on to me all the time, because, as she said, the more I had on the less likely I was to get hurt. And Devoe was there, and he was saying that it wasn't fair; that the football rules distinctly said that players should wear only one sweater. But nobody paid any attention to him. And after a bit, when I was so covered with sweaters that I was round, like a big ball, the Dean whistled and we got into line - that is," said Sydney doubtfully, "it was sort of like a line. There was the President and Neil Fletcher and I on one side, and all the others, at least thirty of them, on the other. It didn't seem quite fair, but I didn't like to object for fear they'd say I was afraid."

"Well, you *did* have the nightmare," said Mills. "Then what?"

"The other side got into a bunch, and I knew they were playing tackle-back, although of course they weren't really; they just all stood together. And I didn't see any ball, either. Then some one yelled 'Smash 'em up!' and they started for us. At that Neil - at least I think it was Neil - and Prexy - I mean the President - took hold of me, lifted me up like a bag of potatoes, and hurled me right at the other crowd. I went flying through the air, turning round and round and round, till I thought I'd never stop. Then there was an awful bump, I yelled 'Down!' at the top of my lungs - and woke up. I was on the floor."

Mills laughed, and Sydney took breath.

"At first I didn't know what had happened. Then I remembered the dream, and all on a sudden, like a flash of lightning,
it occurred to me that *that* was the way to stop tackle-back!"

"That? What?" asked Mills, looking puzzled.

"Why, the bag of potatoes act," laughed Sydney. "I jumped
up, lighted the gas, got pencil and paper and went back to bed
and worked it out. And here it is."

He drew a carefully folded slip of paper from his pocket and
handed it across to Mills. The diagram, just as the head coach
received it, is reproduced here.

Mills studied it for a minute in silence; once he grunted; once
he looked wonderingly up at Sydney. In the end he laid it
beside him on the desk.

"I think you've got it, Burr," he said quietly, "I think you've
got it, my boy. If this works out the way it should, your
nightmare will be the luckiest thing that's happened at Erskine
for several years. Draw your chair up here - I beg your pardon;
I forgot. I'll do the moving myself." He placed his own chair
beside Sydney's and handed the diagram to him. "Now just go
over this, will you; tell me just what your idea is."

Sydney, still excited over the night's happenings, drew a ready
pencil from his pocket, and began rather breathlessly:

"I've placed the Robinson players in the positions that our
second team occupies for the tackle-tandem. Full-back, left
tackle, and right half, one behind the other, back of their
guard-tackle hole. Now, as the ball goes into play their tandem
starts. Quarter passes the ball to tackle, or maybe right half,
and they plunge through our line. That's what they would do

if we couldn't stop them, isn't it?"

"They would, indeed," answered Mills grimly. "About ten yards through our line!"

"Well, now we place our left half in our line between our guard and tackle, and put our full-back behind him, making a tandem of our own. Quarter stands almost back of guard, and the other half over here. When the ball is put in play our tandem starts at a jump and hits the opposing tandem just at the moment their quarter passes the ball to their runner. In other words, we get through on to them before they can get under way. Our quarter and right half follow up, and, unless I'm away off on my calculations, that tackle-tandem is going to stop on its own side of the line."

Sydney paused and awaited Mills's opinion. The latter was silent a moment. Then -

"Of course," he said, "you've thought of what's going to happen to that left half?"

"Yes," answered Sydney, "I have. He's going to get most horribly banged up. But he's going to stop the play."

"Yes, I think he is - if he lives," said Mills with a grim smile. "The only objection that occurs to me this moment is this: Have we the right to place any player in a position like this where the punishment is certain to be terrific, if not absolutely dangerous?"

"I've thought of that, too," answered Sydney readily. "And I don't believe we - er - you have."

"Well, then I think our play's dished at the start."

"Why, not a bit, sir. Call the players up, explain the thing to them, and tell them you want a man for that position."

"Ah, ask for volunteers, eh?"

"Yes, sir. And you'll have just as many, I'll bet, as there are men!"

Mills smiled.

"Well, it's a desperate remedy, but I believe it's the only one, and we'll see what can be done. By the way, I observe that you've taken left half for the victim?"

"Yes, sir; that's Neil Fletcher. He's the fellow for it, I think."

"But I thought he was a friend of yours," laughed Mills.

"So he is; that's why I want him to get it; he won't ask anything better. And he's got the weight and the speed. The fellow that undertakes it has got to be mighty quick, and he's got to have weight and plenty of grit. And that's Neil."

"Yes, I think so too. But I don't want him to get used up and not be able to kick, for we'll need a field-goal before the game is over, if I'm not greatly mistaken. However, we can find a man for that place, I've no doubt. For that matter, we must find two at least, for one will never last the game through."

"I suppose not. I - I wish I had a chance at it," said Sydney longingly.

"I wish you had," said Mills. "I think you'd stand all the punishment Robinson would give you. But don't feel badly that you can't play; as long as you can teach the rest of us the game you've got honor enough."

Sydney flushed with pleasure, and Mills took up the diagram again.

"Guard and tackle will have their work cut out for them," he said. "And I'm not sure that left end can't be brought into it, too. There's one good feature about Robinson's formation, and that is we can imagine where it's coming as long as it's a tandem. If we stop them they'll have to try the ends, and I don't think they'll make much there. Well, we'll give this a try to-morrow, and see how it works. By the way, Burr," he went on, "you can get about pretty well on your crutches, can't you?"

"Yes," Sydney answered.

"Good. Then what's to prevent you from coming out to the field in the afternoons and giving us a hand with this? Do you think you could afford the time?"

Sydney's eyes dropped; he didn't want Mills to see how near the tears were to his eyes.

"I can afford the time all right," he answered in a voice that, despite his efforts, was not quite steady, "if you really think I can be of any use."

Perhaps Mills guessed the other's pleasure, for he smiled gently as he answered:

"I don't think; I'm certain. You know this play better than I do; it's yours; you know how you want it to go. You come out and look after the play; we'll attend to the players. And then, if we find a weak place in it, we can all get together and remedy it. But you oughtn't to try and wheel yourself out there and back every day. You tell me what time you can be ready each afternoon and I'll see that there's a buggy waiting for you."

"Oh, no, really!" Sydney protested. "I'd rather not! I can get to the field and back easily, without getting at all tired; in fact, I need the exercise."

"Well, if you're certain of that," answered the coach. "But any time you change your mind, or the weather's bad, let me know. If you can, I'd like you to come around here again this evening. I'll have Devoe and the coaches here, and we'll talk this - this 'antidote' over again. Well, good-by."

Sydney swung himself to the door, followed by Mills, and got into his tricycle.

"About eight this evening, if you can make it, Burr," said Mills. "Good-by." He stood at the door and watched the other as he trundled slowly down the street.

"Poor chap!" he muttered. And then: "Still, I'm not so sure that he's an object of pity. If he hasn't any legs worth mentioning, the Almighty made it up to him by giving him a whole lot of brains. If he can't get about like the rest of us he's a great deal more contented, I believe, and if he can't play football he can show others how to. And," he added, as he returned to his desk, "unless I'm mistaken, he's done it to-day. Now to mail this list and then for the 'antidote'!"

That night in Mills's room the assembled coaches and captain talked over Sydney's play, discussed it from start to finish, objected, explained, argued, tore it to pieces and put it together again, and in the end indorsed it. And Sydney, silent save when called on for an explanation of some feature of his discovery, sat with his crutches beside his chair and listened to many complimentary remarks; and at ten o'clock went back to Walton and bed, only to lie awake until long after the town-clock had struck midnight, excited and happy.

Had you been at Erskine at any time during the following two weeks and had managed to get behind the fence, you would have witnessed a very busy scene. Day after day the varsity and the second fought like the bitterest enemies; day after day the little army of coaches shouted and fumed, pleaded and scolded; and day after day a youth on crutches followed the struggling, panting lines, instructing and criticizing, and happier than he had been at any time in his memory.

For the "antidote," as they had come to call it, had been tried and had vindicated its inventor's faith in it. Every afternoon the second team hammered the varsity line with the tackle-tandem, and almost every time the varsity stopped it and piled it up in confusion. The call for volunteers for the thankless position at the front of the little tandem of two had resulted just as Sydney had predicted. Every candidate for varsity honors had begged for it, and some half dozen or more had been tried. But in the end the choice had narrowed down to Neil, Paul, Gillam, and Mason, and these it was that day after day bore the brunt of the attack, emerging from each pile-up beaten, breathless, scarred, but happy and triumphant. Two weeks is short time in which to teach a new play, but Mills and the others went bravely and confidently to work, and it seemed that success was to justify the attempt; for three days before the Robinson game the varsity had at last attained perfection in the new play, and the coaches dared at last to hope for victory.

But meanwhile other things, pleasant and unpleasant, had happened, and we must return to the day which had witnessed the inception of Sydney Burr's "antidote."

CHAPTER XVI

ROBINSON SENDS A PROTEST

When Sydney left Mills that morning he trundled himself along Elm Street to Neil's lodgings in the hope of finding that youth and telling him of his good fortune. But the windows of the first floor front study were wide open, the curtains were hanging out over the sills, and from within came the sound of the broom and clouds of dust. Sydney turned his tricycle about in disappointment and retraced his path, through Elm Lane, by the court-house with its tall white pillars and green shutters, across Washington Street, the wheels of his vehicle rustling through the drifts of dead leaves that lined the sidewalks, and so back to Walton. He had a recitation at half-past ten, but there was still twenty minutes of leisure according to the dingy-faced clock on the tower of College Hall. So he left the tricycle by the steps, and putting his crutches under his arms, swung himself into the building and down the corridor to his study. The door was ajar and he thrust it open with his foot.

"Please be careful of the paint," expostulated a voice, and Sydney paused in surprise.

"Well," he said; "I've just been over to your room looking for you."

"Have you? Sorry I wasn't - Say, Syd, listen to this." Neil dragged a pillow into a more comfortable place and sat up. He had been stretched at full length on the big window-seat.

"Here it is in a nutshell," he continued, waving the paper he was reading.

"'First a signal, then a thud,
And your face is in the mud.
Some one jumps upon your back,
And your ribs begin to crack.
Hear a whistle. "Down!" That's all.
'Tis the way to play football.'"

"Pretty good, eh? Hello, what's up? Your face looks as bright as though you'd polished it. How dare you allow your countenance to express joy when in another quarter of an hour I shall be struggling over my head in the history of Rome during the second Punic War? But there, go ahead; unbosom yourself. I can see you're bubbling over with delightful news. Have they decided to abolish the Latin language? Or has the faculty been kidnaped? Have they changed their minds and decided to take me with 'em to New Haven to-morrow? Come, little Bright Eyes, out with it!"

Sydney told his good news, not without numerous eager interruptions from Neil, and when he had ended the latter executed what he called a "Punic war-dance." It was rather a striking performance, quite stately and impressive, for when one's left shoulder is made immovable by much bandaging it is difficult, as Neil breathlessly explained, to display *abandon* - the latter spoken through the nose to give it the correct French pronunciation.

"And, if you're not good to me," laughed Sydney, "I'll get back at you in practise. And I'm to be treated with respect, also, Neil; in fact, I believe you had better remove your cap when you see me."

"All right, old man; cap - sweater - anything! You shall be treated with the utmost deference. But seriously, Syd, I'm awfully glad. Glad all around; glad you've made a hit with the play, and glad you've found something to beat Robinson with.

Ralph Henry Barbour

Now tell me again about it; where do I come in on it?"

And so Sydney drew a chair up to the table and drew more diagrams of the new play, and Neil looked on with great interest until the bell struck the half-hour, and they hurried away to recitations.

The next day the varsity and substitutes went to New Haven. Neil wasn't taken along, and so when the result of the game reached the college - Yale 40, Erskine 0 - he was enabled to tell Sydney that it was insanity for Mills and Devoe to expect to do anything without his (Neil's) services.

"If they will leave me behind, Syd, what can they hope for save rout and disaster? Of course, I realize that I could not have played, but my presence on the side-line would have inspired them and have been very, very helpful. I'm sure the score would have been quite different, Syd."

"Yes," laughed the other; "say fifty to nothing."

"Your levity and disrespect pains me," mourned Neil.

But despite the overwhelming nature of the defeat, Mills and Devoe and the associate coaches found much to encourage them. No attempt had been made to try the new defensive play, but Erskine had managed to make her distance several times. The line had proved steady and had borne the severe battering of the Yale backs without serious injury. The Purple's back-field had played well; Paul had been in his best form, Gillam had gained ground quite often through Yale's wings, and Mason, at full-back, had fought nobly. The ends had proved themselves quick and speedy in getting down under punts, and several of the Blue's tries around end had been nipped ingloriously in the bud. But, when all was said, the principal honors of the contest had fallen to Ted Foster, Erskine's plucky quarter, whose handling of the team had been wonderful, and whose catching and running back of punts had more than once turned the tide of battle. On the whole,

Erskine had put up a good, fast, well-balanced game; had displayed plenty of grit, had shown herself well advanced in team-play, and had emerged practically unscathed from a hard-fought contest.

On Monday Neil went into the line-up for a few minutes, displacing Paul at left-half, but did not form one of the heroic tandem. His shoulder bothered him a good deal for the first minute or two, but after he had warmed up to the work he forgot about it and banged it around so that Simson was obliged to remonstrate and threaten to take him out. On the second's twenty yards Neil was given a chance at a goal from placement, and, in spite of his right shoulder, and to the delight of the coaches, sent the leather over the bar. When he turned and trotted back up the field he almost ran over Sydney, who was hobbling blithely about the gridiron on his crutches.

"Whoa!" cried Neil. "Back up! Hello, Board of Strategy; how do you find yourself?"

"That was fine, Neil," said Sydney.

"What?"

"That goal."

"Glad you liked it. I was beastly nervous," he laughed. "Had no idea I could do it. It's so different trying goals in a game; when you're just off practising it doesn't seem to bother you."

"Oh, you'll do. Gale is growling like a bear because they took him out."

"Is he?" asked Neil. "I'm sorry. Do you know whether he stands a good show for the game? Have you heard Mills or Devoe say anything about it?" Sydney shook his head.

"I'm afraid Gillam's got us both boxed," continued Neil. "As for me, I suppose they'll let me in because I can sometimes kick a goal, but I'm worried about Paul. If he'd only - Farewell, they are lining up again."

"I don't believe Gale will get into the Robinson game," thought Sydney as he took himself toward the side-line. "He seems a good player, but - but you never can tell what he's going to do; half the time he just sort of slops around and looks as though he was doing a favor by playing. I can't see why Neil likes him so well; I suppose it's because he's so different. Maybe he's a better sort when you know him real well."

After practise was ended and the riotous half-hour in the locker-house was over, Neil found himself walking back to the campus with Sydney and Paul. Paul entertained a half-contemptuous liking for Sydney. To Neil he called him "the crip," but when in Sydney's presence was careful never to say anything to wound the boy's feelings - an act of consideration rather remarkable for Paul, who, while really kind at heart, was oftentimes careless about the sensibilities of others. This afternoon Paul was evidently downcast, too downcast to be even cross.

"Well, I guess it's all up with me," he said as they passed through the gate and started down Williams Street toward college. "I'm glad you're back, chum, but I can see my finish."

"Nonsense," said Neil, "you'll be back to-morrow. Gillam is putting up a star game, and that's a fact; but your weight will help you, and if you buckle down for the next few days you'll make it all right."

But Paul refused to be comforted and remained silent and gloomy all the way home. Knowing how Paul had set his heart upon making the varsity for the Robinson game, Neil began to be rather worried himself. He felt, unnecessarily of course, in a measure responsible for the crowning of his friend's ambition. When he had prevailed on Paul to relinquish the idea of going to Robinson, he had derided the possibility of Paul failing to make the Erskine team; and now that possibility was rapidly assuming the appearance of a probability. Certainly the fault was Paul's, and not his; but the thought contained small comfort.

Next day's practise, in preparation for Erskine's last game before the Robinson contest, proved Paul's fears far from groundless. Gillam, Neil, and Mason started work when the line-up was formed, and Paul looked on heart-brokenly from the bench. It was not until Neil had failed twice and succeeded once at field-goals, and Gillam had been well hammered by the second's tandem plays, that Paul secured a chance. Then Neil was taken out and his friend put in.

Neil wrapped a frayed gray blanket about his shoulders and reflected ruefully upon events. He knew that he had played poorly; that he had twice tied up the play by allowing his thoughts to wander; that his end-running had been slow, almost listless, and that his performance at goal-kicking had been miserable. He had missed two tries from placement, one on the twenty yards and another on the twenty-seven, and had only succeeded at a drop-kick by the barest of margins. He couldn't even lay the blame on his injured shoulder, for that was no longer a factor in his playing; the bandages were off and only a leather pad remained to remind him of the incident. No, he had simply worried his stupid head over Paul's troubles, he told himself, and had thereby disappointed the coaches, the captain, and himself. Simson found him presently and sent him trotting about the field, an exercise that worked some of his gloom off and left him in a fairly cheerful frame of mind when he ran up the locker-house steps.

But at dinner he found that his appetite had almost deserted him. Simson observed him gravely, and after the meal was over questioned closely. Neil answered rather irritably, and the trainer's uneasiness increased; but he only said:

"Go to bed early to-night and lay off to-morrow. You'll be

better by Monday. And you might take a walk to-morrow afternoon; go off into the country somewhere; see if you can't find some one to go with you. How's the shoulder? No trouble there, is there?"

"No, there's no trouble anywhere; I just wasn't hungry."

"Well, you do what I've told you and you'll get your appetite back, my boy."

Neil turned away frowning and took himself to his lodging, feeling angry with Simson because he was going to keep him off the field, and angry with himself because - oh, just because he was.

But Neil was not the only person concerned with Erskine athletics who was out of sorts that night. A general air of gloom had pervaded the dinner-table. Mills had been even silenter than usual; the three other coaches present had been plainly worried, and Simson, in spite of his attempts to keep the conversation cheerful, had showed that he too was bothered about something. A bomb-shell had landed in the Erskine camp and had exploded in Mills's quarters.

On the front steps Neil met Cowan. The two always nodded to each other, but to-night Neil's curt salutation went unheeded. Cowan, with troubled face, hurried by him and went up the street toward Mills's rooms.

"Every one's grouchy to-night," muttered Neil. "Even Cowan looks as though he was going to be shot."

Meanwhile the athletic authorities of Erskine and the coaches were met in extraordinary session. They were considering a letter which had arrived that afternoon from Collegetown. In the letter Robinson announced her protest of Thomas L. Cowan, right-guard on the Erskine football team, on the score of professionalism.

"It just means," wailed Foster, who had brought the tidings to Neil and Paul, "that it's all over with us. I don't know what Cowan has to say, but I'll bet a - I'll bet my new typewriter! - that Robinson's right. And with Cowan gone from right-guard, where are we? We haven't the ghost of a show. The only fellow they can play in his place is Witter, and he's a pygmy. Not that Witter doesn't know the position, for he does; but he's too light. Was there ever such luck? What good is Burr's patent, double-action, self-inking, cylindrical, switch-back defense if we haven't got a line that will hold together long enough for us to get off our toes? It - it's rotten luck, that's what it is."

And the varsity quarter-back groaned dolorously.

"But what does Cowan say?" asked Neil.

"Don't ask me," said Foster. "I don't know what he says, and I don't believe it will matter. He's got professional written all over his face."

"But he played last year," said Paul. "Why didn't they protest him then?"

"I'll pass again," answered Foster. "Maybe they hadn't discovered it - whatever it is - then; maybe -"

"Listen!" said Neil.

Some one stamped up the steps and entered the front door. Foster looked questioningly at Neil.

"Cowan?" he whispered. Neil nodded.

Foster sprang to the study door and threw it open. The light from the room fell on the white and angry countenance of the right-guard.

"Cowan," said Foster, "for heaven's sake, man, tell us about it!

Is it all right?"

But Tom Cowan only glared as he passed on up the stairs.

CHAPTER XVII

A PLAN AND A CONFESSION

Robinson's protest set forth succinctly that Cowan had, three years previous, played left tackle on the football team of a certain academy - whose right to the title of academy was often questioned - and had received money for his services. Dates and other particulars were liberally supplied, and the name and address of the captain of the team were given. Altogether, the letter was discouragingly convincing, and neither the coaches, the captain, nor the athletic officers really doubted the truth of the charge.

Professor Nast, the chairman of the Athletic Committee, blinked gravely through his glasses and looked about the room.

"You've sent for Mr. Cowan?" he asked.

"Yes," Mills answered; "he ought to be here in a minute. How in the world was he allowed to get on to the team?"

"Well, his record was gone over, as we believed, very thoroughly year before last," said Professor Nast; "and we found nothing against him. I think - ah - it seems probable that he unintentionally misled us. Perhaps he can - ah - explain."

When, however, Cowan faced the group of grave-faced men it was soon evident that explanations were far from his thoughts.

He had heard enough before the summons reached him to enable him to surmise what awaited him, and when Professor Nast explained their purpose in calling him before them, Cowan only displayed what purported to be honest indignation. He stormed violently against the Robinson authorities and defied them to prove their charge. Mills listened a while impatiently and then interrupted him abruptly.

"Do you deny the charge, Cowan, or don't you?" he asked.

"I refuse to reply to it," answered Cowan angrily. "Let them think what they want to; I'm not responsible to them. It's all revenge, nothing else. They tried to get me to go to them last September; offered me free coaching, and guaranteed me a position on the team. I refused. And here's the result."

Professor Nast brightened and a few of those present looked relieved. But Mills refused to be touched by Cowan's righteousness, and asked brusquely:

"Never mind what their motive is, Cowan. What we want to know is this: Did you or did you not accept money for playing left tackle on that team? Let us have an answer to that, please."

"It's absurd," said Cowan hotly. "Why, I only played three games -"

"Yes or no, please," said Mills.

For an instant Cowan's gaze faltered. He glanced swiftly about the room and read only doubt or antagonism in the faces there. He shrugged his broad shoulders and replied sneeringly:

"What's the good? You're all down on me now; you wouldn't believe me if I told you."

"We're not all down on you," answered Mills. Professor Nast interrupted.

"One moment, Mr. Mills. I don't think Mr. Cowan understands the - ah - the position we are in. Unless you can show to our satisfaction that the charge is untrue, Mr. Cowan, we shall be obliged, under the terms of our agreement with Robinson, to consider you ineligible. In that case, you could not, of course, play against Robinson; in fact, you would not be admitted to any branch of university athletics. Now, don't you think that the best course for you to follow is to make a straightforward explanation of your connection with the academy in question? We are not here to judge the - ah - ethics of your course; only to decide as to whether or no you are eligible to represent the college in athletics."

Cowan arose from his seat and with trembling fingers buttoned his overcoat. His brow was black, but when he spoke, facing the head coach and heedless of the rest, he appeared quite cool.

"Ever since practise began," he said, "you have been down on me and have done everything you could to get rid of me. No matter what I did, it wasn't right. Whether I'm eligible or ineligible, I'm done with you now. You may fill my place - if you can; I'm out of it. You'll probably be beaten; but that's your affair. If you are, I sha'n't weep over it."

He walked to the door and opened it.

"It's understood, I guess, that I've resigned from the team?" he asked, facing Mills once more.

"Quite," said the latter dryly.

"All right. And now I don't mind telling you that I did get paid for playing with that team. I played three games and took money every time. It isn't a crime and I'm not ashamed of it, although to hear you talk you'd think I'd committed murder. Good-night, gentlemen."

He passed out. Professor Nast blinked nervously.

"Dear me," he murmured, "dear me, how unpleasant!"

Mills smiled grimly, and, rising, stretched his limbs.

"I think what we have left to do won't take very long. I hardly think that it is necessary for me to reply to the accusations brought by the gentleman who has just left us."

"No, let's hear no more of it," said Preston. "I propose that we reply to Robinson to-night and have an end of the business. To-morrow we'll have plenty to think of without this," he added grimly.

The reply was written and forwarded the next day to Robinson, and the following announcement was given out at Erskine:

> The Athletic Committee has decided that Cowan is not eligible to represent the college in the football game with Robinson, and he has been withdrawn. A protest was received from the Robinson athletic authorities yesterday afternoon, and an investigation was at once made with the result stated. The loss of Cowan will greatly weaken the team, it is feared, but that fact has not been allowed to influence the committee. The decision is heartily concurred in by the coaches, the captain, and all officials, and, being in line with Erskine's policy of purity in athletics, should have the instant indorsement of the student body.
>
> H.W. NAST, *Chairman.*

The announcement, as was natural, brought consternation, and for several days the football situation was steeped in gloom. Witter and Hurst were seized upon by the coaches and drilled in the tactics of right-guard. As Foster had said, Witter, while he was a good player, was light for the position. Hurst, against whom no objection could be brought on the ground of weight, lacked experience. In the end Witter proved first choice, and Hurst was comforted with the knowledge that he was practically certain to get into the game before the whistle sounded for the last time.

Meanwhile Artmouth came and saw and conquered to the tune of 6-0, profiting by the news of Cowan's withdrawal and piling their backs through Witter, Hurst, and Brown, all of whom took turns at right-guard. The game was not encouraging from the Erskine point of view, and the gloom deepened. Foster declared that it was so thick during the last half of the contest that he couldn't see the backs. Neil saw the game from the bench, and Paul, once more at left-half, played an excellent game; but, try as he might, could not outdo Gillam. When it was over Neil declared the honors even, but Paul took a less optimistic view and would not be comforted.

All the evening, save for a short period when he went upstairs to sympathize with Cowan, he bewailed his fate into Neil's ears. The latter tried his best to comfort him, and predicted that on Monday Paul would find himself in Gillam's place. But he scarcely believed it himself, and so his prophecies were not convincing.

"What's the good of being decent?" asked Paul dolefully. "I wish I'd gone to Robinson."

"No, you don't," said Neil. "You'd rather sit on the side-line at Erskine than play with a lot of hired sluggers."

"Much you know about it," Paul growled. "If I don't get into the Robinson game I'll - I'll leave college."

"But what good would that do?" asked Neil.

"I'd go somewhere where I'd stand a show. I'd go to Robinson or one of the smaller places."

"I don't think you'd do anything as idiotic as that," answered Neil. "It'll be hard luck if you miss the big game, but you've got three more years yet. What's one? You're certain to stand the best kind of a show next year."

"I don't see how. Gillam doesn't graduate until 1903."

"But you can beat him out for the place next year. All you need is more experience. Gillam's been at it two years here. Besides, it would be silly to leave a good college just because you couldn't play on the football team. Don't be like Cowan and think football's the only thing a chap comes here for."

"They've used him pretty shabbily," said Paul.

"That's what Cowan thinks. I don't see how they could do anything else."

"He's awfully cut up. I'm downright sorry for him. He says he's going to pack up and leave."

"And he's been trying to make you do the same, eh?" asked Neil. "Well, you tell him I'm very well satisfied with Erskine and haven't the least desire to change."

"You?" asked Paul.

"Certainly. We hang together, don't we?"

Paul grinned.

"You're a good chap, chum," he said gratefully. "But -" relapsing again into gloom - "you're not losing your place on the team, and you don't know how it feels. When a fellow's set his heart on it -"

"I think I do know," answered Neil. "I know how I felt when my shoulder went wrong and I thought I was off for good and all. I didn't like it. But cheer up, Paul, and give 'em fits Monday. Slam 'round, let yourself loose; show 'em what you can do. Down with Gillam!"

"Oh, I dare say," muttered Paul dejectedly.

Neil laid awake a long time that night; he was full of sympathy for his room-mate. With him friendship meant more than it does to the average boy of nineteen, and he was ready and eager to do anything in his power that would insure Paul's getting into the Robinson game. The trouble was that he could think of nothing, although he lay staring into the darkness, thinking and thinking, until Paul had been snoring comfortably across the room for more than an hour.

The next afternoon, Sunday, Neil, obeying the trainer's instructions, went for a walk. Paul begged off from accompanying him, and Neil sought Sydney. That youth was delighted to go, and so, Neil alternately pushing the tricycle and walking beside it while Sydney propelled it himself, the two followed the river for several miles into the country. The afternoon was cold but bright, and being outdoors was a pleasure to any healthy person. Neil forgot some of his worries and remembered that, after all, he was still a boy; that football is not the chief thing in college life, and that ten years hence it would matter little to him whether he played for his university against her rival or looked on from the bench. And it was that thought that suggested to him a means of sparing Paul the bitter disappointment that he dreaded.

The plan seemed both simple and feasible, and he wondered why he had not thought of it before. To be sure, it involved the sacrificing of an ambition of his own; but to-day, out here among the pines and beeches, with the clear blue sky overhead and the eager breeze bringing the color to his cheeks, the sacrifice seemed paltry and scarcely a sacrifice at all. He smiled to himself, glad to have found the solution of Paul's trouble, which was also his own; but suddenly it occurred to him that perhaps he had no right to do what he contemplated. The ethics were puzzling, and presently he turned to Sydney, who had been silently and contentedly wheeling himself along across the road, and sought his counsel.

"Look here, Syd, you're a level-headed sort of chump. Give me your valuable opinion on this, will you? Now - it's a supposititious case, you know - here are two fellows, A and B, each trying for the same - er - prize. Now, supposing A has just about reached it and B has fallen behind; and supposing I -"

"Eh?" asked Sydney.

"Yes, I meant A. Supposing A knows that B is just as deserving of the prize as he is, and that - that he'll make equally as good use of it. Do you follow, Syd?"

"Y - yes, I think so," answered the other doubtfully.

"Well, now, the question I want your opinion on is this: Wouldn't it be perfectly fair for A to - well, slip a cog or two, you know -"

"Slip a cog?" queried Sydney, puzzled.

"Yes; that is," explained Neil, "play off a bit, but not enough for any of the fellows to suspect, and so let B get the plum?"

"Well," answered Sydney, after a moment's consideration, "it sounds fair enough -"

"That's what I think," said Neil eagerly.

"But maybe A and B are not the only ones interested. How about the conditions of the contest? Don't they require that each man shall do his best? Isn't it intended that the prize shall go to the one who really is the best?"

"Oh, well, in a manner, maybe," answered Neil. He was silent a moment. The ethics was more puzzling than ever. Then: "Of course, it's only a supposititious case, you understand, Syd," he assured him earnestly.

"Oh, of course," answered the other readily. "Hadn't we better turn here?"

The journey back was rather silent. Neil was struggling with his problem, and Sydney, too, seemed to have something on his mind. When the town came once more into view around a bend in the road Sydney interrupted Neil's thoughts.

"Say, Neil, I've got a - a confession to make." His cheeks were very red and he looked extremely embarrassed. Neil viewed him in surprise.

"A confession? You haven't murdered the Dean, have you?"

"No. It - it's something rather different. I don't believe that it will make any difference in our - our friendship, but - it might."

"It won't," said Neil. "Now, fire ahead."

"Well, you recollect the day you found me on the way from the field and pushed me back to college?"

"Of course. Your old ice-wagon had broken down and I -"

"That's it," interrupted Sydney, with a little embarrassed laugh. "It hadn't."

"What hadn't? Hadn't what?"

"The machine; it hadn't broken down."

"But I saw it," exclaimed Neil. "What do you mean, Syd?"

"I mean that it hadn't really broken down, Neil. I - the truth is I had pried one of the links up with a screw-driver."

Neil stared in a puzzled way.

"But - what for?" he asked.

"Don't you understand?" asked Sydney, shame-faced. "Because I wanted to know you, and I thought if you found me there with my machine busted you'd try to fix it; and I'd make your acquaintance. It - it was awfully dishonest, I know," muttered Sydney at the last.

Neil stared for a moment in surprise. Then he clapped the other on the shoulder and laughed uproariously.

"Oh, to think of guileless little Syd being so foxy!" he cried. "I wouldn't have believed it if any one else had told me, Syd."

"Well," said Sydney, very red in the face, but joining in the laughter, "you don't mind?"

"Mind?" echoed Neil, becoming serious again, "why of course I don't. What is there to mind, Syd? I'm glad you did it, awfully glad." He laid his arm over the shoulders of the lad on the seat. "Here, let me push a while. Queer you should have cared that much about knowing me; but - but I'm glad." Suddenly his laughter returned.

"No wonder that old fossil in the village thought it was a queer sort of a break," he shouted. "He knew what he was talking about after all when he suggested cold-chisels, didn't he?"

CHAPTER XVIII

NEIL IS TAKEN OUT

The Tuesday before the final contest dawned raw and wet. The elms in the yard *drip-dripped* from every leafless twig and a fine mist covered everything with tiny beads of moisture. The road to the field, trampled by many feet, was soft and slippery. Sydney, almost hidden beneath rain-coat and oil-skin hat, found traveling hard work. Ahead of him marched five hundred students, marshaled by classes, a little army of bobbing heads and flapping mackintoshes, alternately cheering and singing. Dana, the senior-class president, strode at the head of the line and issued his commands through a big purple megaphone.

Erskine was marching out to the field to cheer the eleven and to practise the songs that were to be chanted defiantly at the game. Sydney had started with his class, but had soon been left behind, the rubber tires of the machine slipping badly in the mud. Presently the head of the procession, but dimly visible to him through the mist, turned in at the gate, the monster flag of royal purple, with its big white E, drooping wet and forlorn on its staff. They were cheering again now, and Sydney whispered an accompaniment behind the collar of his coat:

"Erskine! Erskine! Erskine! Rah-rah-rah, rah-rah-rah, rah-rah-rah! Erskine! Erskine! Erskine!"

Suddenly footsteps sounded behind him and the tricycle went

Ralph Henry Barbour

forward apparently of its own volition. Sydney turned quickly and saw Mills's blue eyes twinkling down at him.

"Did I surprise you?" laughed the coach.

"Yes, I thought my wheel had suddenly turned into an automobile."

"Hard work for you, I'm afraid. You should have let me send a trap for you," said Mills. "Never mind those handles. Put your hands in your pockets and I'll get you there in no time. What a beast of a day, isn't it?"

"Y - yes," answered Sydney, "I suppose it is. But I rather like it."

"Like it? Great Scott! Why?"

"Well, the mist feels good on your face, don't you think so? And the trees down there along the railroad look so gray and soft. I don't know, but there's something about this sort of a day that makes me feel good."

"Well, every one to his taste," Mills replied. "By the way, here's something I cut out of the Robinson Argus; thought you'd like to see it." He drew a clipping from a pocketbook and gave it to Sydney, who, shielding it from the wet, read as follows:

Erskine, we hear, is crowing over a wonderful new play which she thinks she has invented, and with which she expects to get even for what happened last year. We have not seen the new marvel, of course, but we understand that it is called a "close formation." It is safe to say that it is an old play revamped by Erskine's head coach, Mills. Last year Mills discovered a form of guards-back which was heralded to the four corners of the earth as the greatest play ever seen. What happened to it is still within memory. Consequently we are not greatly alarmed over the latest production of his fertile brain. Robinson can, we think, find a means of solving any puzzle that Erskine can put together.

"They're rather hard on you," laughed Sydney as he returned the clipping.

"I can stand it. I'm glad they haven't discovered that we are busy with a defense for their tackle-tandem. If we can keep that a secret for a few days longer I shall be satisfied."

"I do hope it will come up to expectations," said Sydney doubtfully. "Now that the final test is drawing near I'm beginning to fear that maybe we - maybe we're too hopeful."

"I know," answered Mills. "It's always that way. When I first began coaching I used to get into a regular blue funk every year just before the big game; used to think that everything was going wrong, and was firmly convinced until the whistle sounded that we were going to be torn to pieces and scattered to the winds. It's just nerves; you get used to it after a while. As for the new defense for tackle-tandem, it's all right. Maybe it won't stop Robinson altogether, but it's the best thing that a light team can put up against a heavy one playing Robinson's game; and I think that it's going to surprise her and worry her quite a lot. Whether it will keep her from scoring on the tackle play remains to be seen. That's a good deal to hope for. If we'd been able to try the play in a game with another college we would know more about what we can do with it. As it is, we only know that it will stop the second and that theoretically it is all right. We'll be wiser on the 23d.

"Frankly, though, Burr," he continued, "as a play I don't like it. That is, I consider it too hard on the men; there's too much brute force and not enough science and skill about it; in fact, it isn't football. But as long as guards-back and tackle-back formations are allowed it's got to be played. It was a mistake in ever allowing more than four men behind the line. The natural formation of a football team consists of seven players in the line, and when you begin to take one or two of those players back you're increasing the element of physical force and lessening the element of science. More than that, you're playing into the hands of the anti-football people, and giving them further grounds for their charge of brutality.

"Football's the noblest game that's played, but it's got to be played right. We did away with the old mass-play evil and then promptly invented the guards-back and the tackle-back. Before long we'll see our mistake and do away with those too; revise the rules so that the rush-line players can not be drawn back. Then we'll have football as it was meant to be played; and we'll have a more skilful game and one of more interest both to the players and spectators." Mills paused and then asked:

"By the way, do you see much of Fletcher?"

"Yes, quite a bit," answered Sydney. "We were together for two or three hours yesterday afternoon."

"Indeed? And did you notice whether he appeared in good spirits? See any signs of worry?"

"No, not that I recall. I thought he appeared to be feeling very cheerful. I know we laughed a good deal over - over something."

"That's all right, then," answered the coach as they turned in through the gate and approached the locker-house. "I had begun to think that perhaps he had something on his mind that troubled him. He seemed a bit listless yesterday at practise. How about his studies? All right there, is he?"

"Oh, yes. Fletcher gets on finely. He was saying only a day or two ago that he was surprised to find them going so easily."

"Well, don't mention our talk to him, please; he might start to worrying, and that's what we don't want, you know. Perhaps he'll be in better shape to-day. We'll try him in the 'antidote.'"

But contrary to the hopes of the head coach, Neil showed no improvement. His playing was slow, and he seemed to go at things in a half-hearted way far removed from his usual dash and vim. Even the signals appeared to puzzle him at times, and more than once Foster turned upon him in surprise.

"Say, what the dickens is the matter with you, Neil?" he whispered once. Neil showed surprise.

"Why, nothing; I'm all right."

"Well, I'm glad you told me," grumbled the quarter-back, "for I'd never have guessed it, my boy."

Before the end of the ten minutes of open practise was over Neil had managed to make so many blunders that even the fellows on the seats noticed and remarked upon it. Later, when the singing and cheering were over and the gates were closed behind the last marching freshman, Neil found himself in hot water. The coaches descended upon him in a small army, and he stood bewildered while they accused him of every sin in the football decalogue. Devoe took a hand, too, and threatened to put him off if he didn't wake up.

"Play or get off the field," he said. "And, hang it all, man, look intelligent, as though you liked the game!"

Neil strove to look intelligent by banishing the expression of bewilderment from his face, and stood patiently by until the last coach had hurled the last bolt at his defenseless head - defenseless, that is, save for the head harness that was dripping rain-drops down his neck. Then he trotted off to the line-up with a queer, half-painful grin on his face.

"I guess it's settled for me," he said to, himself, as he rubbed his cold, wet hands together. "Evidently I sha'n't have to play off to give Paul his place; I've done it already. I suppose I've been bothering my head about it until I've forgotten what I've been doing. I wish though -" he sighed - "I wish it hadn't been necessary to disgust Mills and Bob Devoe and all the others who have been so decent and have hoped so much of me. But it's settled now. Whether it's right or wrong, I'm going to play like a fool until they get tired of jumping on me and just yank me out in sheer disgust.

"Simson's got his eagle eye on me, the old ferret! And he will have me on the hospital list to-morrow, I'll bet a dollar. He'll say I've gone 'fine' and tell me to get plenty of sleep and stay outdoors. And the doctor will give me a lot of nasty medicine. Well, it's all in the bargain. I'd like to have played in Saturday's game, though; but Paul has set his heart on it, and if he doesn't make the team he'll have seven fits. It means more to him than it does to me, and next fall will soon be here. I can wait."

"*Fletcher! Wake up, will you?*"

Foster was glaring at him angrily. The blood rushed into Neil's face and he leaped to his position. Even Ted Foster's patience had given out, Neil told himself; and he, like all the rest, would have only contempt for him to-morrow. The ball was wet and slimy and easily fumbled. Neil lost it the first time it came into his hands.

"Who dropped that ball?" thundered Mills, striding into the back-field, pushing players left and right.

"I did," answered Neil, striving to meet the coach's flashing eyes and failing miserably.

"You did? Well, do it just once more, Fletcher, and you'll go off! And you'll find it hard work getting back again, too. Bear that in mind, please." He turned to the others. "Now get together here! Put some life into things! Stop that plunging right here! If the second gets another yard you'll hear from me!"

"First down; two yards to gain!" called Jones, who was acting as referee.

The second came at them again, tackle-back, desperately, fighting hard. But the varsity held, and on the next down held again.

"That's better," cried Mills.

"Use your weight, Baker!" shrieked one of the second's coaches, slapping the second's left-guard fiercely on the back to lend vehemence to the command.

"Center, your man got you that time," cried another. "Into him now! Throw him back! Get through!"

Ten coaches were raving and shrieking at once.

"Signal!" cried the second's quarter, Reardon. The babel was hushed, save for the voice of Mills crying:

"Steady! Steady! Hold them, varsity!"

"*44 - 64 - 73 - 81!*" came Reardon's muffled voice. Then the second's backs plunged forward. Neil and Gillam met them with a crash; cries and confusion reigned; the lines shoved and heaved; the backs hurled themselves against the swaying group; a smothered voice gasped "Down!" the whistle shrilled.

"Varsity's ball!" said the referee. "First down!"

The coaches began their tirades anew. Mills spoke to Foster aside. Then the lines again faced each other. Foster glanced back toward Neil.

"*14 - 12 - 34 - 9!*" he sang. It was a kick from close formation. Neil changed places with full-back. He had forgotten for the moment the role he had set himself to play, and only thought of the ball that was flying toward him from center. He would do his best. The pigskin settled into his hands and he dropped it quickly, kicking it fairly on the rebound. But the second was through, and the ball banged against an upstretched hand and was lost amidst a struggling group of players. In a moment it came to light tightly clutched by Brown of the second eleven.

"I don't have to make believe," groaned Neil. "Fate's playing squarely into my hands."

Five minutes later the leather went to him for a run outside of left tackle. He never knew whether he tried to do it or really stumbled, but he fell before the line was reached, and in a twinkling three of the second eleven were pushing his face into the muddy turf. The play had lost the varsity four yards. Mills glared at Neil, but said not a word. Neil smiled weakly as he went back to his place.

"I needn't try any more," he thought wearily. "He's made up his mind to put me off."

A minute later the half ended. When the next one began Paul Gale went in at left half-back on the varsity. And Neil, trotting to the locker-house, told himself that he was glad, awfully glad, and wished the tears wouldn't come into his eyes.

CHAPTER XIX

ON THE EVE OF BATTLE

Neil was duly pronounced "fine" by the trainer, dosed by the doctor, and disregarded by the coaches. Mills, having finally concluded that he was too risky a person for the line-up on Saturday, figuratively labeled him "declined" and passed him over to Tassel, head coach of the second eleven. Tassel displayed no enthusiasm, for a good player gone "fine" is at best a poor acquisition, and of far less practical value than a poor player in good condition. It made little difference to Neil what team he belonged to, for he was prohibited from playing on Wednesday, and on Thursday the last practise took place and he was in the line-up but five minutes. On that day the students again marched to the field and practised their songs and cheers. Despite the loss of Cowan and the lessening thereby of Erskine's chance of success, enthusiasm reigned high. Perhaps their own cheers raised their spirit, for two days before the game the college was animated by a totally unwarranted degree of hopefulness that amounted almost to confidence. The coaches, however, remained carefully pessimistic and took pains to see that the players did not share the general hopefulness.

"We may win," said Mills to them after the last practise, "but don't think for a moment that it's going to be easy. If we do come out on top it will be because every one of you has played as he never dreamed he could play. You've got to play your own positions perfectly and then help to play each other's.

Remember what I've said about team-play. Don't think that your work is done when you've put your man out; that's the time for you to turn around and help your neighbor. It's just that eagerness to aid the next man, that stand-and-fall-together spirit, that makes the ideal team. I don't want to see any man on Saturday standing around with his hands at his sides; as long as the ball's in play there's work for every one. Don't cry 'Down' until you can't run, crawl, wriggle, roll, or be pulled another inch. And if you're helping the runner don't stop pulling or shoving until there isn't another notch to be gained. Never mind how many tacklers there are; the ball's in play until the whistle sounds. And, one thing more, remember that you're not going to do your best because I tell you to, or because if you don't the coaches will give you a wigging, or because a lot of your fellows are looking on. You're going to fight your hardest, fight until the last whistle blows, fight long after you can't fight any more, because you're wearing the Purple of old Erskine and can't do anything else but fight!"

The cheer that followed was good to hear. There was not a fellow there that didn't feel, at that moment, more than a match for any two men Robinson could set up against him. And many a hand clenched involuntarily, and many a player registered his silent vow to fight, as Mills had said, long after he couldn't fight any more, and, if it depended on him, win the game for old Erskine.

On Friday afternoon the men were assembled in the gymnasium and were drilled in signals and put through a hard examination in formations. Afterward several of the coaches addressed them earnestly, touching each man on the spot that hurt, showing them where they failed and how to remedy their defects, but never goading them to despondency.

"I should be afraid of a team that was perfect the day before the game," said Preston; "afraid that when the real struggle came they'd disappoint me. A team should go into the final contest with the ability to play a little better than it has played at any time during the season; with a certain amount of power in reserve. And so I expect to-morrow to see almost all of the faults that we have talked of eliminated. I expect to see every man do that little better that means so much. And if he does he'll make Mr. Mills happy, he'll make all the other coaches happy, he'll make his captain and himself happy, and he'll make the college happy. And he'll make Robinson unhappy!"

Then the line-up that was to start the game was read. Neil, sitting listlessly between Paul and Foster, heard it with a little ache at his heart. He was glad that Paul was not to be disappointed, but it was hard to think that he was to have no part in the supreme battle for which he had worked conscientiously all the fall, and the thought of which had more than once given him courage to go on when further effort seemed impossible.

"Stone, Tucker, Browning, Stowell, Witter, Carey, Devoe, Foster, Gale -"

"Good for you, Paul," whispered Neil. Then he sighed as the list went on -

"Gillam, Mason."

Then a long string of substitutes was read. Neil's name was among these, but that fact meant little enough.

"Every man whose name has been read report at eleven to-morrow for lunch. Early to bed is the rule for every one to-night, and I want every one to obey it." Mills paused; then he went on in softer tones: "Some of you are disappointed. Some of you have worked faithfully - you all have, for that matter - only to meet with disappointment to-day. But we can't put you all in the line-up; I wish we could. But to those who have tried so hard and so honestly for positions in to-morrow's game, and who have of necessity been left out, I can only offer the sympathy of myself and the other coaches, and of the other players. You have done your share, and it no doubt seems hard that you are to have no better share in the final test. But let me tell you that even though you do not play against Robinson, you have nevertheless done almost as much toward defeating her as though you faced her to-morrow. It's the season's work that counts - the long, hard preparation - and in that you've had your place and done your part well. And for that I thank you on behalf of myself, on behalf of the coaches who have been associated with me, and on behalf of the college. And now I am going to ask you fellows of the varsity to give three long Erskines, three-times-three, and three long 'scrubs' on the end!"

And they were given not once, but thrice. And then the scrub lustily cheered the varsity, and they both cheered Mills and Devoe and Simson and all the coaches one after another. And when the last long-drawn "Erskine" had died away Mills faced them again.

"There's one more cheer I want to hear, fellows, and I think you'll give it heartily. In to-morrow's game we are going to use a form of defense that will, I believe, enable us to at least render a good account of ourselves. And, as most of you know, this defense was thought out and developed by a fellow who, although unfortunately unable to play the game himself, is nevertheless one of the finest football men in college. If we win to-morrow a great big share of the credit will be due to that man; if we lose he still will have done as much as any two of us. Fellows, I ask for three cheers for Burr!"

Mills led that cheer himself and it was a good one. The pity of it was that Sydney wasn't there to hear it.

The November twilight was already stealing down over the campus when Neil and Paul left the gymnasium and made their way back to Curtis's. Paul was highly elated, for until the line-up had been read he had been uncertain of his fate. But his joy was somewhat dampened by the fact that Neil had failed to make the team.

"It doesn't seem just right for me to go into the game, chum, with you on the side-line," he said. "I don't see what Mills is thinking of! Who in thunder's to kick for us?"

"I guess you'll be called on, Paul, if any field-goals are needed."

"I suppose so, but - hang it, Neil, I wish you were going to play!"

"Well, so do I," answered Neil calmly; "but I'm not, and so that settles it. After all, they couldn't do anything else, Paul, but let me out. I've been playing perfectly rotten lately."

"But - but what's the matter? You don't look stale, chum."

"I feel stale, just the same," answered Neil far from untruthfully.

"But maybe you'll get in for a while; you're down with the subs," said Paul hopefully.

"Maybe I will. Maybe you'll get killed and Gillam'll get killed and a few more'll get killed and they'll take me on. But don't you worry about me; I'm all right."

Paul looked at him as though rather puzzled.

"By Jove, I don't believe you care very much whether you play or don't," he said at last. "If it had been me they'd let out I'd simply gone off into a dark corner and died."

"I'm glad it wasn't you," answered Neil heartily.

"Thunder! So'm I!"

The college in general had taken Neil's deflection philosophically after the first day or so of wonderment and dismay. The trust in Mills was absolute, and if Mills said Fletcher wasn't as good as Gale for left half-back, why, he wasn't; that was all there was about it. There was one person in college, however, who was not deceived. Sydney Burr, recollecting Neil's "supposititious case," never doubted that Neil had purposely sacrificed himself for his room-mate. At first he was inclined to protest to Neil, even to go the length of making Mills cognizant of the real situation; but in the end he kept his own counsel, doubtful of his right to interfere. And, in some way, he grew to think that Paul was not in the dark; that he knew of Neil's plan and was lending his sanction to it; that, in fact, the whole arrangement was a conspiracy in which both Neil and Paul shared equally. In this he did Paul injustice, as he found out later.

He went to Neil's room that Friday night for a few minutes and found Paul much wrought up over the disappearance of Tom Cowan. Cowan's room looked as though a cyclone had struck it, Paul declared, and Cowan himself was nowhere to be found.

"I'll bet he's done what he said he'd do and left," said Paul. But Sydney had seen him but an hour or so before at commons, and Paul set out to hunt him up.

"I know you chaps don't like him," he said; "but he's been mighty decent to me, and I don't want to seem to be going back on him just now when he's so down on his luck. I'll be back in a few minutes."

Sydney found Neil quite cheerful and marveled at it. He himself was oppressed by a nervousness that couldn't have been worse had he been due to face Robinson's big center the next day. He feared the "antidote" wouldn't work right; he feared Robinson had found out all about it and had changed their offense; he feared a dozen evils, and Neil was kept busy comforting him. At nine o'clock Paul returned without tidings of Cowan, and Sydney said good-night.

"I don't believe I'll go out to the field to-morrow," he said half seriously. "I'll stay in my room and listen to the cheering. If it sounds right toward the end of the game I'll know that things have gone our way."

"You won't be able to tell anything of the sort," said Neil, "for the fellows are going to cheer just as hard if we lose as they would had we won. Mills insists on that, and what he says goes this year."

"That's so," said Paul; "and it's the way it ought to be. If ever a team needs cheering and encouragement it's when things are blackest, and not when it's winning."

"And so, you see, you'll have to go to the field, Syd," said Neil as he followed the other out to the porch. "By Jove, what a night, eh? I never saw so many stars, I believe. Well, we'll have a good clear day for the game and a good turf underfoot. Good-night, Syd."

"Good-night," answered the other. Then, sorrowfully, "I do wish you were going to play, Neil."

"Thanks, Syd; but don't let that keep you awake. Good-night!"

The room-mates chatted in a desultory way for half an hour longer and then prepared for bed. Paul was somewhat nervous and excited, and displayed a tendency to stop short in the middle of removing a stocking to gaze blankly before him for whole minutes at a time. Once he stood so long on one leg with his trousers half off that Neil feared he had gone to sleep, and so brought him back to a recollection of the business in hand by shying a boot at him.

As for Neil, he was untroubled by nervousness. He believed Erskine was going to win. For the rest, the eve of battle held no exciting thoughts for him. He could neither win the game nor lose it; he was merely a spectator, like thousands of others; only he would see the contest from the players' bench instead of the big new stand that half encircled the field.

But despite the feeling of aloofness that possessed and

Ralph Henry Barbour

oppressed him, sleep did not come readily. For a long time he heard Paul stirring about restlessly across the little bedroom and the occasional cheers of some party of patriotic students returning to their rooms across the common. His brain refused to stop its labors; and, in fact, kept busily at them long after he had fallen asleep. He dreamed continually, a ceaseless stream of weird, unpleasant visions causing him to turn and toss all through the night and leaving him when dawn came weary and unrefreshed.

Out of doors the early sun was brushing away the white frost. The sky was almost devoid of clouds, and the naked branches of the elms reached upward unswayed by any breeze. It was an ideal day, that 23d of November, bright, clear, and keen. Nature could not have been kinder to the warriors who, in a few short hours, were to meet upon the yellowing turf, nor to the thousands who were to assemble and cheer them on to victory - or defeat.

CHAPTER XX

COWAN BECOMES INDIGNANT

Breakfast at the training-table that morning was a strange meal, to which the fellows loitered in at whatever hour best pleased them. Many showed signs of restless slumber, and the trainer was as watchful as an old hen with a brood of chickens. For some there were Saturday morning recitations; those who were free were sent out to the field at ten o'clock and were put through a twenty-minute signal practise. Among these were Neil and Paul. A trot four times around the gridiron ended the morning's work, and they were dismissed with orders to report at twelve o'clock for lunch.

Neil, Paul, and Foster walked back together, and it was the last that suggested going down to the depot to see the arrival of the Robinson players. So they turned down Poplar Street to Main and made their way along in front of the row of stores there. The village already showed symptoms of excitement. The windows were dressed in royal purple, with here and there a touch of the brown of Robinson, and the sidewalk already held many visitors, while others were invading the college grounds across the street. Farther on the trio passed the bicycle repair-shop. In front of the door, astride an empty box, sat the proprietor, sunning himself and keeping a careful watch on the village happenings. With a laugh Neil left his companions and ran across the street.

"Good-morning," he said. The little man on the box looked

up inquiringly but failed to recognize his tormentor.

"Mornin'," he grunted suspiciously.

"I wanted to tell you," said Neil gravely, "that your diagnosis was correct, after all."

"Hey?" asked the little man querulously.

"Yes, it *was* a cold-chisel that did it," said Neil. "You remember you said it was."

"Cold-chisel? Say, what you talkin' -" Then a light of recognition sprang into his weazened features. "You're the feller that owes me a quarter!" he cried shrilly, scrambling to his feet.

Neil was off on the instant. As the three went on toward the station the little man's denunciations followed them:

"You come back here an' pay me that quarter! If I knew yer name I'd have ther law on yer! But I know yer face, an' I'll -"

"His name's Legion," called Ted Foster over his shoulder.

"Hey? What?" shrieked the repair man.

"Legion!"

"I don't know what you say, but I'll report that feller ter th' authorities!"

Then a long whistle broke in upon the discussion, and the three rushed for the station platform.

From the vantage-point of a baggage-truck they watched the Robinson players and the accompanying contingent descend from the train. There were twenty-eight of the former, heavily built, strapping-looking fellows, and with them a small army of coaches, trainers, and supporters. Neil dug his elbow against Paul.

"Look," he said, "there's your friend Brill."

And sure enough, there was the Robinson coach who had visited the two at Hillton a year before and tried to get them to go to the rival college.

"If you'd like to make arrangements for next year, Paul," Neil whispered mischievously, "now's your time."

But Paul grinned and shook his head.

The players and most of the coaches tumbled into carriages and were taken out to Erskine Field for a short practise, and the balance of the arrivals started on foot toward the hotel. The three friends retraced their steps. Luckily, the proprietor of the bicycle repair-shop was so busy looking over the strangers that they passed unseen in the little stream. There remained the better part of an hour before lunch-time, and they found themselves at a loss for a way to spend the time. Foster finally went off to his room, as he explained airily, "to dash off a letter on his typewriter," a statement that was greeted with howls of derision from the others, who, for want of a better place, went into Butler's bookstore and aimlessly looked over the magazines and papers.

It was while thus engaged that Paul heard his name spoken, and turned to find Mr. Brill smilingly holding out his hand.

"I thought I wasn't mistaken," the Robinson coach said as they shook hands. "And isn't that your friend Fletcher over there?"

Neil heard and came over, and the three stood and talked for a few minutes. Mr. Brill seemed well pleased with the football outlook.

"I'll wager you gentlemen will regret not coming to us after to-day's game is over," he laughed. "I hear you've got something up your sleeve."

"We have," said Neil.

"So I heard. What's the nature of it?"

"It's muscle," answered Neil gravely.

The coach laughed. "Of course, if it's a secret, I don't want to hear it. But I think you're safe to get beaten, secret or no secret, eh?"

"Nonsense!" said Paul. "You won't know what struck you when we get through with you."

Mr. Brill laughed good-naturedly but didn't look alarmed.

"By the way," he said, "I saw one of your players a while ago - Cowan - the fellow we protested. He seemed rather sore."

"Where was he?" asked Paul eagerly.

"In a drug-store down there toward the next corner. Have your coaches found a good man for his place?"

"Oh, yes, it wasn't hard to fill," answered Neil. "Witter's got it."

"Witter? I don't think I've heard of him."

"No, he's not famous - yet; you'll know him better later on."

Paul was plainly anxious to go in search of Cowan, and so they bade the Robinson coach good-by. Out on the sidewalk Neil turned a troubled face toward his friend.

"Say, Paul, Cowan knows all about the 'antidote,' doesn't he?"

"Why, yes, I suppose so; he's seen it played."

"And he knows the signals, too, eh?"

"Of course. Why?"

"Well, I've been wondering whether - You heard what Brill said - that Cowan was feeling sore? Well, do you suppose he'd be mean enough to - to -"

"By thunder!" muttered Paul. Then: "No, I don't believe that Cowan would do a thing like that. I don't think he's a - a traitor!"

"Well, you know him better than I do," said Neil, "and I dare say you're right. Only - only I wish we could be certain."

"I'll find him," answered Paul determinedly. "You wait here for me; or, no, I may have to hunt; I'll see you at lunch. I'll find out all right."

He was off on the instant. As he had told Neil, he didn't believe that Cowan would reveal secrets to Brill or any other of the Robinson people; but - well, he realized that Cowan was feeling very much aggrieved, and that he might in his present state of mind do what in a saner moment he would not consider. At the drug-store he was told that Cowan had left a few minutes before. The only place that Paul could think of where Cowan was likely to be was his room, so thither he went. He found the deposed guard engaged in replacing certain of his pictures and ornaments which had been taken down.

"Hello!" he said. "Thought you'd cut my acquaintance too."

"Nonsense," answered Paul, "I've been trying to find you ever since last night. Where've you been?"

"Oh, just knocking around. I got back late last night."

"I was afraid you had left college. You know you said you might."

"I know. Well, I've changed my mind. I guess I'll stay on until recess anyway; maybe until summer. What's the use going anywhere else? If I went to Robinson I couldn't play; Erskine would protest me. I wish to goodness I'd had sense enough to let that academy team go hang! Only I needed some money, and it seemed a good way to make it. After all, there wasn't anything dishonest about it!"

"N - no," said Paul.

"Well, was there?" Cowan demanded, turning upon him fiercely. Paul shook his head.

"No, there wasn't. Only, of course, you'd ought to have remembered that it disqualified you here." Cowan looked surprised.

"My, but you're getting squeamish!" he said. "The first thing you know you'll be as bad as Fletcher." There was a moment's silence. "What does he say about it?" Cowan asked carelessly.

"Who, Neil? Oh, he - he sympathizes with you," answered Paul vaguely. "Says it's awfully hard lines, but doesn't think the committee could do anything else."

"Humph!"

"By the way," said Paul, recollecting his errand, "I met Brill of Robinson a while ago. He said he'd seen you."

"Yes," grunted Cowan. "I'd like to punch him. Made believe he was all cut up over my being put off. Why - why it was he that knew about that academy business! Last September he tried to get me to go to Robinson; offered me anything I wanted, and I refused. After all a - a fellow's got some loyalty! He asked all sorts of questions as to whether I was eligible or not, and I - I don't know what made me, but I told him about taking that money for playing tackle on that old academy team. He said that wouldn't matter any. But after I decided not to go to Robinson he changed his tune; said he wasn't sure but that I was ineligible!"

"He's a cad," said Paul."

"And then to-day he tried to get sympathetic, but I shut him up mighty quick. I told him I knew well enough he was the one who had started the protest, and offered to punch his nose if he'd come over back of the stores; but he wouldn't," added Cowan aggrievedly.

"You - you didn't let out anything to him that would - er - help them in the game, did you?" asked Paul, studying the floor with great attention.

"Let out anything?" asked Cowan in puzzled tones. "What do you -" He put down the picture he held and faced Paul, the blood dying his face. "Look here, Paul, what do you mean by that?"

"Why, why -"

"You want to know if I turned traitor? If I gave away our signals or something like that, eh?" There was honest indignation in his voice and a trace of pain, and Paul regretted his suspicions on the instant.

"Oh, come now, old man," he began, "what I meant -"

"Now let me tell you something, Gale," said Cowan. "I may not be so nice as you and Fletcher and Devoe and a lot more of your sort, but I'm not an out-and-out rascal and traitor! And I didn't think you'd put that on me, by Jove! I've no love for some of the fellows in this college, nor for Mills, and I wouldn't care if we got beaten -" He paused. "Yes, I would, too; I want Robinson to get done up so hard that they'll throw that cheat Brill out of there. But I want you to understand right here and now that I'm not cad enough to sell signals."

"I beg your pardon, Tom," said Paul earnestly. "I didn't think it of you. Only, when Brill said he'd seen you and that you were feeling sore, we - I -"

"Oh, so it was Fletcher that suspected it, was it?" demanded Cowan.

"No more than I," answered Paul stoutly. "We neither of us really thought you'd turn traitor, but I was afraid that, feeling the way you naturally would, you might thoughtlessly say something that Brill could make use of. That's all"

Cowan looked doubtful for a moment, then he sniffed.

"Well, all right," he said finally. "Forget it."

"You're going out to the game, aren't you?" Paul asked.

"Yes, I guess so. What's Fletcher think of being laid off?"

"Well, he doesn't seem to mind it as I thought he would. I - I don't know quite what to make of him. It almost seems that he's - well, glad of it!"

"Huh! You've got another guess, my friend."

"How's that? What do you mean?"

"Nothing much; only I guess I've got better eyes than you," responded Cowan with a grin. After a pause during which he rearranged the objects on the mantel-shelf to his satisfaction, he turned to Paul again:

"Say, do you think Fletcher and I could get on together if - well, if we knew each other better?"

"I'm sure you could," answered Paul eagerly.

"Well, I think I'd like to try it. He - he's not a bad sort of a chap. Only maybe he wouldn't care to - er -"

"Oh, yes, he would," answered Paul. "You'll see, Tom."

"Well, maybe so. Going? Good luck to you. I'll see you on the field."

Paul hurried around the long curve of Elm Street toward Pearson's boarding-house, where the players were already gathering for luncheon. He found Neil on the steps and dragged him off and down to the gate.

"It's all right," he said. "I found him and asked him, and I wish I hadn't. He was awfully cut up about it; seemed hurt to think I could suspect such a thing. Though, really, I didn't quite suspect, you know."

"I'm sorry we hurt his feelings," said Neil. "It was a bit mean of me to suggest it."

"He's going to stay for a while," went on Paul. "And - and - Look here, chum, don't you think that if - er - you tried you could get to like him better? From something he said to-day I found out that he thinks you're a good sort and he'd like to get on with you. Maybe if we kind of looked after him we could - oh, I don't know! But you see what I mean?"

"Yes, I see what you mean," replied Neil thoughtfully. "And maybe we'd get on better if we tried again. Anyhow, Paul, you ask him down to the room some night and - and we'll see."

"Thanks," said Paul gratefully. "And now let's get busy with the funeral baked beans - I mean meats. Gee, I've got about as much appetite as a fly! I - I wish the game was over with!"

Ralph Henry Barbour

"So do I," answered Neil, as with a sigh he listlessly followed his chum into the house.

CHAPTER XXI

THE "ANTIDOTE" IS ADMINISTERED

High up against a fair blue sky studded with fleecy clouds streamed a banner of royal purple bearing in its center a great white E - a flare of intense color visible from afar over the topmost branches of the empty elms, and a beacon toward which the stream of spectators set their steps. In the tower of College Hall the old bell struck two o'clock, and the throngs at the gates of Erskine Field moved faster, swaying and pushing past the ticket-takers and streaming out onto the field toward the big stands already piled high with laughing, chattering humanity. Under the great flag stretched a long bank of somber grays and black splashed thickly with purple, looking from a little distance as though the big banner had dripped its dye on to the multitude beneath. Opposite, the rival tiers of crowded seats were pricked out lavishly with the rich but less brilliant brown, while at the end of the enclosure, where the throngs entered, a smaller stand flaunted the two colors in almost equal proportions.

And between stretched a smooth expanse of russet-hued turf ribbed with white lines that glared in the afternoon sunlight.

The college band, augmented for the occasion from the ranks of the village musicians, played blithely; some twelve thousand persons talked, laughed, or shouted ceaselessly; and the cheering sections were loudly contending for vocal supremacy. And suddenly on to this scene trotted a little band of men in black sweaters with purple 'E's, nice new canvas trousers, and purple and black stockings; and just as suddenly the north stand arose and the Robinson cheers were blotted out by a mighty chorus that swept from end to end of the structure and thundered impressively across the field:

"*Erskine! Erskine! Erskine! Rah-rah-rah, rah-rah-rah, rah-rah-rah! Erskine! Erskine! Erskine!*"

It was repeated over and over, and might, perhaps, have been sounding yet had not the Robinson players, sturdy, brown-clad youths, ambled onto the field. Then it was Robinson's turn to make a noise, and she made it; there's no doubt about that.

"*Rah-rah-rah! Robinson! Rah-rah-rah! Robinson! Rah-rah-rah! Robinson! Robinson! Robinson!*"

The substitutes of both teams retired to the benches and the players who were to start the game warmed up. Over near the east goal three Erskine warriors were trying - alas, not very successfully! - to kick the ball over the cross-bar; they were Devoe and Paul and Mason. Nearer at hand Ted Foster was personally conducting a little squad around the field by short stages, and his voice, shrilly cheerful, thrilled doubting supporters of the Purple hopefully. Robinson's players were going through much the same antics at the other end of the gridiron, and there was a business-like air about them that caused many an Erskine watcher to scent defeat for his college.

The cheers had given place to songs, and the leader of the band faced the occupants of the north stand and swung his baton vigorously. Presumably the band was playing, but unless you had been in its immediate vicinity you would never have known it. Many of the popular airs of the day had been refitted with new words for the occasion. As poetic compositions they were not remarkable, but sung with enthusiasm by several hundred sturdy voices they answered the purpose. Robinson replied in kind, but in lesser volume, and the preliminary battle, the war of voices, went on until three persons, a youth in purple, a youth in brown, and a man in everyday attire, met in the middle of the field and watched a coin spin upward in the sunlight and fall to the ground. Then speedily the contesting forces took their position, the linesmen and timekeeper hurried forward, and the great stands were almost stilled.

Erskine had the ball and the west goal. Stowell poised the pigskin to his liking and drew back. Devoe shouted a last word of caution. The referee, a well-known football player and coach, raised his whistle.

"Are you ready, Erskine? All ready, Robinson?"

Then the whistle shrilled, the timekeeper's watch clicked, the ball sped away, and the game had begun.

The brown-clad skirmishers leaped forward to oppose the invaders, while the pigskin, slowly revolving, arched in long flight toward the west goal. It struck near the ten-yard line and the wily Robinson left half let it go; but instead of rolling over the goal-line it bumped erratically against the left post and bobbed back to near the first white line. The left half was on it then like a flash, but the Erskine forwards were almost upon him and his run was only six yards long, and it was Robinson's ball on her ten-yard line. The north stand was applauding vociferously this stroke of fortune. If Erskine could get possession of the ball now she might be able to score; but her coaches,watching intently from the side-line, knew that only the veriest fluke could give the pigskin to the Purple. And meanwhile, with hearts beating a little faster than usual, they awaited the first practical test of the "antidote."

Robinson lined up quickly. Left tackle dropped from the line, and taking a position between full-back and right half, formed the center of the tandem that faced the tackle-guard hole on the right. Left half stood well back, behind quarter, ready to oppose any Erskine players who managed to get around the left of their line. The full-back who headed the tandem was a notable line-bucker, although his weight was but 172 pounds. The left tackle, Balcom, tipped the scales at 187, while the third member of the trio was twenty pounds lighter. Together they represented 525 pounds.

Opposed to them were Gillam and Mason, whose combined weight was 312 pounds. Gillam stood between left-guard and tackle, with Mason, his hands on the other's shoulders, close behind.

The Robinson quarter stared for an instant with interest at the opposing formation, and the full-back, crouched forward ready to plunge across the little space that divided him from the opponents' territory, looked uneasy. Then the quarter stooped behind the big center.

"*Signal!*" he called. "*12 - 21 - 212!*"

The ball came back to him. At the same instant the tandem moved forward, the Erskine guard and tackle engaged the opposing guard and tackle, and Gillam and Mason shot through the hole, the former with head down and a padded shoulder presented to the enemy, and the latter steadying him and hurling him forward. Then two things happened at the same moment; the ball passed from quarter to tackle, and Gillam and the leader of the tandem came together.

The shock of that collision was plainly heard on the side-lines. For an instant the tandem stopped short. Then superior weight told, and it moved forward again, reenforced by quarter and right end; but simultaneously the Erskine quarter and left half made themselves felt back of Mason and Gillam, and then chaos reigned. The entire forces of each side were in the play, and for nearly half a minute the swaying mass moved inch by inch, first forward, then backward, the Robinson left tackle refusing to believe that their famous play was for once a failure and so clinging desperately to the ball, the center of a veritable maelstrom of panting, struggling players. Then the whistle sounded and the dust of battle cleared away. Robinson had gained half a yard.

The north stand cheered delightedly. It had only seen the Robinson tandem stopped in its tracks, and did not know that in the struggle just passed Erskine had used a new and novel defense for the first time on any football field, had vindicated her coaches' faith in it, and brought surprise and dismay to the brown-clad warriors and their adherents. If it had known as much as Mills and Jones and Sydney about the "antidote" it would have shouted itself hoarse.

Gillam trotted back to his place. His extra-padded head-harness and heavy shoulder-pads had brought him forth unscathed. On the side-line the Erskine coaches talked softly to each other, trying hard to look unconcerned, but nevertheless showing their pleasure. Sydney Burr, rather pale, was among them, and was, perhaps, the happiest of all. The bench whereon the substitutes sat was one long grin from end to end. But Robinson was far from being beaten, and the game went on.

Again the tandem was hurled at the same point, and again Gillam met the shock of it. This time the defense worked better, and Robinson lost the half-yard of gain and another half-yard on top of that.

"Six yards to gain," said the score-board. And the purple-decked stand voiced its triumph.

Robinson wisely decided to yield possession of the ball and get away from such a dangerous locality. On the next play she punted and Paul was brought to earth on Robinson's fifty yards. Now was the time for Erskine to test her offensive powers. On the first play, using the close-formation, Gillam slashed a hole between the opposing center and right-guard and Mason went through for two yards. The next play netted them another yard in the same place. Then Paul was given the pigskin for a try outside of right tackle and reeled off four yards more before he was downed. It was quick starting and fast running, and for the moment Robinson was taken off her feet; but the next try ended dismally, for in an attempt to get through the left of the line between guard and tackle Mason was caught and thrown back for a two-yard loss. Another try outside of tackle on that side of the line netted but a bare three feet, and Foster dropped back for a kick. His effort was not very successful, and the ball was Robinson's on her twenty-seven yards.

Now she tried the tackle-tandem on the other side of center, hurling right tackle, followed by left half with the ball, and full-back at the guard-tackle hole. Paul led the defense this time, and again Robinson was brought up all standing. Another try at the same point with like results, and Robinson changed her tactics. With the tandem formation, the ball went to full-back, and with left end and tackle interfering he skirted Erskine's right for seven yards and brought the wearers of the brown to their feet shouting wildly. Perhaps no one was more surprised than Bob Devoe, for it was his end that had been circled. Certainly no one was more thoroughly disgusted than he. The Robinson left end had put him out of the play as neatly as though he had been the veriest tyro. Devoe sized up that youth, set his lips together, and kept his eyes open.

Robinson now had the ball near her thirty-five yards and returned to the tackle-tandem. In two plays she gained two yards, the result of faster playing. Then another try outside of right tackle brought her five yards. Tackle-tandem again, one yard; again, two yards; a try outside of tackle, one yard; Erskine's ball on Robinson's forty-three yards. The pigskin went to Gillam, who got safely away outside Robinson's right end and reeled off ten yards before he was caught. Again he was given the ball for a plunge through right tackle and barely gained a yard. Mason found another yard between left-guard and tackle and Foster kicked. It was poorly done, and the leather went into touch at the twenty-five yards, and once more Robinson set her feet toward the Erskine goal.

So far the playing had all been done in her territory and her coaches were looking anxious. Erskine's defense was totally unlooked for, both as regarded style and effectiveness, and the problem that confronted them was serious. Their team had been perfected in the tackle-tandem play to the neglecting of almost all else. Their backs were heavy and consequently slow when compared with their opponents. To be sure, thus far runs outside of tackle and end had been successful, but the coaches well knew that as soon as Erskine found that such plays were to be expected she would promptly spoil them. Kicking was not a strong point with Robinson this year; at that game her enemy could undoubtedly beat her. Therefore, if the tackle-back play didn't work what was to be done? There was only one answer: Make it! There was no time or opportunity now to teach new tricks; Robinson must stand or fall by tackle-tandem. And while the coaches were arriving at this conclusion, White, their captain and quarter-back, had already reached it.

He placed the head of the tandem nearer the line, put the tackle at the head of it, and hammered away again. Mills, seeing the move, silently applauded. It was the one way to strengthen the tandem play, for by starting nearer the line the tandem could possibly reach it before the charging opponents got into the play. Momentum was sacrificed and an instant of time gained, and, as it proved, that instant of time meant a difference of fully a yard on each play. Had the two Erskine warriors whose duty it was to hurl themselves against the tandem been of heavier weight it is doubtful if the change made would have greatly benefited their opponents; but, as it was, the two forces met about on Robinson's line, and after the first recoil the Brown was able to gain, sometimes a bare eighteen inches, sometimes a yard, once or twice three or four.

And now Robinson took up her march steadily toward the Purple's goal. The backs plowed through for short distances; Gillam and Paul bore the brunt of the terrific assaults heroically; the Erskine line fell back foot by foot, yard by yard; and presently Robinson crossed the fifty-five-yard line and emerged into Erskine territory. Here there was a momentary pause in her conquering invasion. A fumble by the full-back allowed Devoe to get through and fall on the ball.

Erskine now knifed the Brown's line here and there and shot Gillam and Paul through for short gains and made her distance. Then, with the pigskin back in Robinson territory, Erskine was caught holding and Robinson once more took up her advance. Carey at right tackle weakened and the Brown piled her backs through him. On Erskine's thirty-two yards he gave place to Jewell and the tandem moved its attack to the other side of the line. Paul and Gillam, both pretty well punished, still held out stubbornly. Yard by yard the remaining distance was covered. On her fifteen yards, almost under the shadow of her goal-posts, Erskine was given ten yards for off-side play, and the waning hopes of the breathless watchers on the north stand revived.

But from the twenty-five-yard line the steady rushes went on again, back over the lost ground, and soon, with the half almost gone, Robinson placed the ball on Erskine's five yards. Twice the tandem was met desperately and hurled back, but on the third down, with her whole back-field behind the ball, Robinson literally mowed her way through, sweeping Paul and Mason, and Gillam and Foster before her, and threw Bond over between the posts with the ball close snuggled beneath him.

The south stand leaped to its feet, blue flags and streamers fluttered and waved, and cheers for Robinson rent the air until long after the Brown's left half had kicked a goal. Then the two teams faced each other again and the Robinson left end got the kick-off and ran it back fifteen yards. Again the battering of the tackle-tandem began, and Paul and Gillam, nearly spent, were unable to withstand it after the first half dozen plays. Mason went into the van of the defense in place of Gillam, but the Brown's advance continued; one yard, two yards, three yards were left behind.

Mills, watching, glanced almost impatiently at the timekeeper, who, with his watch in hand, followed the battle along the side-line. The time was almost up, but Robinson was back on Erskine's thirty-five yards. But now the timekeeper walked on to the gridiron, his eyes fixed intently on the dial, and ere the ball went again into play he had called time. The lines broke up and the two teams trotted away.

The score-board proclaimed:

Erskine 0, Opponents 6.

CHAPTER XXII

BETWEEN THE HALVES

Neil trotted along at the tail-end of the procession of substitutes, so deep in thought that he passed through the gate without knowing it, and only came to himself when he stumbled up the locker-house steps. He barked his shins and reached a conclusion at the same instant.

At the door of the dressing-room a strong odor of witch-hazel and liniment met him. He squeezed his way past a group of coaches and looked about him. Confusion reigned supreme. Rubbers and trainer were hard at work. Simson's voice, commanding, threatening, was raised above all others, a shrill, imperious note in a rising and falling babel of sound. Veterans of the first half and substitutes chaffed each other mercilessly. Browning, with an upper lip for all the world like a piece of raw beef, mumbled good-natured retorts to the charges brought against him by Reardon, the substitute quarter-back.

"Yes, you really ought to be careful," the latter was saying with apparent concern. "If you let those chaps throw you around like that you may get bruised or broken. I'll speak to Price and ask him to be more easy with you."

"Mmbuble blubble mummum," observed Browning.

"Oh, don't say that," Reardon entreated.

Neil was looking for Paul, and presently he discovered him. He was lying on his back while a rubber was pommeling his neck and shoulders violently and apparently trying to drown him in witch-hazel. He caught sight of Neil and winked one highly discolored eye. Neil examined him gravely; Paul grinned.

"There's a square inch just under your left ear, Paul, that doesn't appear to have been hit. How does that happen?"

Paul grinned more generously, although the effort evidently pained him.

"It's very careless of them, I must say," Neil went on sternly. "See that it is attended to in the next half."

"Don't worry," answered Paul, "it will be." Neil smiled.

"How are you feeling?" he asked.

"Fine," Paul replied. "I'm just getting limbered up."

"You look it," said Neil dryly. "I suppose by the time your silly neck is broken you'll be in pretty good shape to play ball, eh?" Simson hurried up, closely followed by Mills.

"How's the neck?" he asked.

"It's all right now," answered Paul. "It felt as though it had been driven into my body for about a yard."

"Do you think you can start the next half?" asked Mills anxiously.

"Sure; I can play it through; I'm all right now," replied Paul gaily. Mills's face cleared.

"Good boy!" he muttered, and turned away. Neil sped after him.

Ralph Henry Barbour

"Mr. Mills," he called. The head coach turned, annoyed by the interruption.

"Well, Fletcher; what is it?"

"Can't I get in for a while, sir?" asked Neil earnestly. "I'm feeling fine. Gillam can't last the game, nor Paul. I wish you'd let -"

"See Devoe about it," answered Mills shortly. He hurried away, leaving Neil with open mouth and reddening cheeks.

"Well, that's what I get for disappointing folks," he told himself. "Only he needn't have been *quite* so short. What's the good of asking Devoe? He won't let me on. And - but I'll try, just the same. Paul's had his chance and there's no harm now in looking after Neil Fletcher."

He found Devoe with Foster and one of the coaches. The latter was lecturing them forcibly in lowered tones, and Neil hesitated to interrupt; but while he stood by undecided Devoe glanced up, his face a pucker of anxiety. Neil strode forward.

"Say, Bob, get me on this half, can't you? Mills told me to see you," he begged. "Give me a chance, Bob!"

Devoe frowned impatiently and shook his head.

"Can't be done, Neil. Mills has no business sending you to me. He's looking after the fellows himself. I've got troubles enough of my own."

"But if I tell him you're willing?" asked Neil eagerly.

"I'm not willing," said Devoe. "If he wants you he'll put you on. Don't bother me, Neil, for heaven's sake. Talk to Mills."

Neil turned away in disappointment. It was no use. He knew he could play the game of his life if only they'd take him on.

But they didn't know; they only knew that he had been tried and found wanting. There was no time now to test doubtful men. Mills and Devoe and Simson were not to be blamed; Neil recognized that fact, but it didn't make him happy. He found a seat on a bench near the door and dismally looked on. Suddenly a conversation near at hand engaged his attention.

Mills, Jones, Sydney Burr, and two other assistant coaches were gathered together, and Mills was talking.

"The 'antidote's' all right," he was saying decidedly. "If we had a team that equaled theirs in weight we could stop them short; but they're ten pounds heavier in the line and seven pounds heavier behind it. What can you expect? Without the 'antidote' they'd have had us snowed under now; they'd have scored five or six times on us."

"Easy," said Jones. "The 'antidote's' all right, Burr. What we need are men to make it go. That's why I say take Gillam out. He's played a star game, but he's done up now. Let Pearse take his place, play Gale as long as he'll last, and then put in Smith. How about Fletcher?"

"No good," answered Mills. "At least -" He stopped and narrowed his eyes, as was his way when thinking hard.

"I think he'd be all right, Mr. Mills," said Sydney. "I - I know him pretty well, and I know he's the sort of fellow that will fight hardest when the game's going wrong."

"I thought so, too," answered Mills; "but - well, we'll see. Maybe we'll give him a try. Time's up now. - O Devoe!"

"Yes, coming!"

"Here's your list. Better get your men out."

There was a hurried donning of clothing, a renewed uproar.

"All ready, fellows," shouted the captain. "Answer to your names: Kendall, Tucker, Browning, Stowell, Witter, Jewell, Devoe, Gale, Pearse, Mason, Foster."

"There's not much use in talk," said Mills, as the babel partly died away. "I've got no fault to find with the work of any of you in the last half; but we've got to do better in this half; you can see that for yourselves. You were a little bit weak on team-play; see if you can't get together. We're going to tie the score; maybe we're going to beat. Anyhow, let's work like thunder, fellows, and, if we can't do any more, tear that confounded tackle-tandem up and send it home in pieces. We've got thirty-five minutes left in which to show that we're as good if not better than Robinson. Any fellow that thinks he's not as good as the man he's going to line up against had better stay out. I know that every one of you is willing, but some of you appeared in the last half to be laboring under the impression that you were up against better men. Get rid of that idea. Those Robinson fellows are just the same as you - two legs, two arms, two eyes, a nose, and a mouth. Go at it right and you can put them out of the play. Remember before you give up that the other man's just as tuckered as you are, maybe more so. Your captain says we can win out. I think he knows more about it than we fellows on the side-line do. Now go ahead, get together, put all you've got into it, and see whether your captain knows what he's talking about. Let's have a cheer for Erskine!"

Neil stood up on the bench and got into that cheer in great shape. He was feeling better. Mills had half promised to put him in, and while that might mean much or nothing it was ground for hope. He trotted on to the field and over to the benches almost happily.

The spectators were settling back in their seats, and the cheering had begun once more. The north stand had regained its spirit. After all, the game wasn't lost until the last whistle blew, and there was no telling what might happen before that. So the student section cheered and sang, the band heroically strove to make itself heard, and the purple flags tossed and fluttered. The sun was almost behind the west corner of the stand, and overcoat collars and fur neck-pieces were being snuggled into place. From the west tiers of seats came the steady tramp-tramp ofchilled feet, hinting their owners' impatience.

The players took their places, silence fell, and the referee's whistle blew. Robinson kicked off, and the last half of the battle began.

CHAPTER XXIII

NEIL GOES IN

But what a dismal beginning it was!

Pearse, who had taken Gillam's place at right half-back, misjudged the long, low kick, just managed to tip the ball with one outstretched hand as it went over his head, and so had to turn and chase it back to the goal-line. But Mason had seen the danger and was before him. Seizing the bouncing pigskin, he was able to reach the ten-yard line ere the Robinson right end bore him to earth. A moment later the ball went to the other side as a penalty for holding, and it was Robinson's first down on Erskine's twelve yards. Neil, watching intently from the bench, groaned loudly. Stone, beside him, kicked angrily into the turf.

"That settles it," he muttered glumly. "Idiots!"

Pearse it was who met that first fierce onslaught of the Brown's tandem, and he was new to the play; but Mason was behind him, and he was sent crashing into the leader like a ball from the mouth of a cannon. The tandem stopped; a sudden bedlam of voices from the stands broke forth; there were cries of "Ball! Ball!" and Witter flung himself through, rolled over a few times, and on the twenty-yard line, with half the Erskine team striving to pull him on and all the Robinson team trying to pull him back, groaned a faint "Down!" Robinson's tackle had fumbled the pass, and for the moment Erskine's goal was out of danger.

"Line up!" shouted Ted Foster. "Signal!"

The men scurried to their places.

"*49 - 35 - 23!*"

Back went the ball and Pearse was circling out toward his own left end, Paul interfering. The north stand leaped to its feet, for it looked for a moment as though the runner was safely away. But Seider, the Brown's right half, got him about the knees, and though Pearse struggled and was dragged fully five yards farther, finally brought him down. Fifteen yards was netted, and the Erskine supporters found cause for loud acclaim.

"Bully tackle, that," said Neil. Stone nodded.

"Seems to me we can get around those ends," he muttered; "especially the left. I don't think Bloch is much of a wonder. There goes Pearse."

The ends were again worked by the two half-backs and the distance thrice won. The purple banners waved ecstatically and the cheers for Erskine thundered out. Neil was slapping Stone wildly on the knee.

"Hold on," protested the left end, "try the other. That one's a bit lame."

"Isn't Pearse a peach?" said Neil. "Oh, but I wish I was out there!"

"You may get a whack at it yet," answered Stone. "There goes a jab at the line."

"I may," sighed Neil. He paused and watched Mason get a yard through the Brown's left tackle. "Only, if I don't, I suppose I won't get my E."

"Oh, yes, you will. The Artmouth game counts, you know."

"I wasn't in it."

"That's so, you weren't; I'd forgotten. But I think you'll get it, just the - Good work, Gale!" Paul had made four yards outside of tackle, and it was again Erskine's first down on the fifty-five-yard line. The cheers from the north stand were continuous; Neil and Stone were obliged to put their heads together to hear what each other said.

For five minutes longer Erskine's wonderful good fortune continued, and the ball was at length on Robinson's twenty-eight yards near the north side-line. Foster was waving his hand entreatingly toward the seats, begging for a chance to make his signals heard. From across the field, in the sudden comparative stillness of the north stand, thundered the confident slogan of Robinson. The brown-stockinged captain and quarter-back was shouting incessantly:

"Steady now, fellows! Break through! Break through! Smash 'em up!" He ran from one end to the other, thumping each encouragingly on the back, whispering threats and entreaties into their ears. "Now, then, Robinson, let's stop 'em right here!"

Foster, red-faced and hoarse, leaned forward, patted Stowell on the thigh, caught the ball, passed it quickly to Mason as that youth plunged for the line, and then threw himself into the breach, pushing, heaving, fighting for every inch that gave under his torn and scuffled shoes.

"Second down; four to gain!"

Robinson was awake now to her danger. Foster saw the futility of further attempts at the line for the present and called for a run around left end. The ball went to Pearse, but Bloch for once was ready for him, and, getting by Kendall, nailed the runner prettily four yards back of the line to the triumphant paeans of the south stand.

When the teams had again lined up Foster dropped back as though to try a kick for goal, a somewhat difficult feat considering the angle. The Robinson captain was alarmed; he was ready to believe that a team who had already sprung one surprise on him was capable of securing goals from any angle whatever; his voice arose in hoarse entreaty:

"Get through and block this kick, fellows! Get through! Get through!"

"*Signal!*" cried Foster. "*44 - 18 - 23!*"

The ball flew back from Stowell and Foster caught it breast-high. The Erskine line held for a moment, then the blue-clad warriors came plunging through desperately, and had Foster attempted a kick the ball would never have gone ten feet; but Foster, who knew his limitations in the kicking line as well as any one else, had entertained no such idea. The pigskin, fast clutched to Paul's breast, was already circling the Brown's left end. Devoe had put his opponent out of the play, thereby revenging himself for like treatment in the first half, and Pearse, a veritable whirlwind, had bowled over the Robinson left half. There is, perhaps, no prettier play than a fake kick, when it succeeds, and the friends of Erskine recognized the fact and showed their appreciation in a way that threatened to shake the stand from its foundations.

Paul and Pearse were circling well out in the middle of the field toward the Robinson goal, now some thirty yards distant measured by white lines, but far more than that by the course they were taking. Behind them streamed a handful of desperate runners; before them, rapidly getting between them and the goal, sped White, the Robinson captain and quarter. To the spectators a touch-down looked certain, for it was one man against two; the pursuit was not dangerous. But to Paul it seemed at each plunge a more forlorn attempt. So far he had borne more than his share of the punishment sustained by the tackle-tandem defense; he had worked hard on offense since the present half began, and now, wearied and aching in every bone and muscle, he found himself scarce able to keep pace with his interference.

He would have yielded the ball to Pearse had he been able to tell the other to take it; but his breath was too far gone for speech. So he plunged onward, each step slower than that before, his eyes fixed on the farthest white streak. From three sides of the great field poured forth the resonance of twelve thousand voices, triumphant, despairing, appealing, inciting, the very acme of sound.

Yet Paul vows that he heard nothing save the beat of Pearse's footsteps and the awful pounding of his own heart.

On the fifteen-yard line, just to the left of the goal, the critical moment came. White, with clutching, outstretched hands, strove to evade Pearse's shoulder, and did so. But the effort cost him what he gained, for, dodging Pearse and striving to make a sudden turn toward Paul, his foot slipped and he measured his length on the turf; and ere he had regained his feet the pursuit passed over him. Pearse met the first runner squarely and both went down. At the same instant Paul threw up one hand blindly and fell across the last line.

On the north stand hats and flags sailed through the air. The south stand was silent.

Paul lay unmoving where he had fallen. Simson was at his side in a moment. Neil, his heart thumping with joy, watched anxiously from the bench. Presently the group dissolved and Paul emerged between Simson and Browning, white of face and stumbling weakly on his legs, but grinning like a jovial satyr. Mills turned to the bench and Neil's heart jumped into his throat; but it was Smith and not he who struggled feverishly out of his sweater, donned a head-harness, and sped on to the field. Neil sighed and sank back.

"Next time," said Stone sympathetically. But Neil shook his head.

"I guess there isn't going to be any 'next time,'" he said dolefully. "Time's nearly up."

"Not a bit of it; the last ten minutes is longer than all the rest of the game," answered Stone. "I wonder who'll try the goal."

"We've got to have it," said Neil. "Surely Devoe can kick an easy one like that! Why, it's dead in the center!" Stone shook his head.

"I know, but Bob's got a bad way of getting nervous times like this. He knows that if he misses we've lost the game, unless we can manage to score again, which isn't likely; and it's dollars to doughnuts he doesn't come anywhere near it!"

Paul staggered up to the bench, Simson carefully wrapping a blanket about him, and the fellows made room for him a little way from where Neil sat. He stretched his long legs out gingerly because of the aches, sighed contentedly, and looked about him. His eyes fell on Neil.

"Hello, chum!" he said weakly. "Haven't you gone in yet?"

"Not yet," answered Neil cheerfully. "How are you feeling?"

"Oh, I'm - ouch! - I'm all right; a bit sore here and there."

"Devoe's going to kick," said Stone uneasily.

The ball had been brought out, and now Foster was holding it directly in front of the center of the cross-bar. The south stand was cheering and singing wildly in a desperate attempt to rattle the Erskine captain. The latter looked around once, and the Robinson supporters, taking that as a sign of nervousness, redoubled their noise.

Ralph Henry Barbour

"Muckers!" groaned Neil. Stone grinned.

"Everything goes with them," he said.

The referee's hand went down, Devoe stepped forward, the blue-clad line leaped into the field, and the ball sped upward. As it fell Neil turned to Stone and the two stared at each other in doubt. From both stands arose a confused roar. Then their eyes sought the score-board at the west end of the field and they groaned in unison.

"NO GOAL."

"What beastly luck!" muttered Stone.

Neil was silent. Mills and Jones were standing near by and looking toward the bench and Neil imagined they were discussing him. He watched breathlessly, then his heart gave a suffocating leap and he was racing toward the two coaches.

"Warm up, Fletcher."

That was all, but it was all Neil asked for. In a twinkling he was trotting along the line, stretching his cramped legs and arms. As he passed the bench he tried to look unconcerned, but the row of kindly, grinning faces told him that his delight was common property. Paul silently applauded.

Meanwhile the teams had again faced each other. Twelve minutes of play remained and the score-board said: Erskine 5, Opponents 6. Both elevens had made changes. For Erskine, Graham, immense of bulk but slow, had replaced Stowell at center, and Reardon was in Foster's position. Robinson had put in new men at left tackle, right end, and full-back. The game went on again.

Devoe got the kick-off and brought the ball back to his thirty yards; but he was injured when thrown and Bell took his place. Smith and Mason each made two yards around the ends and

Pearse got through left-guard for one. Then a plunge at right tackle resulted disastrously, Mason being forced back three yards, and Smith took the pigskin for a try outside of right tackle. He was stopped easily and Mason kicked. Robinson got the ball on her fifty yards and ran it back to Erskine's forty-three. Once more the tackle-tandem was brought into play. Smith failed to stop it, and the head of the defense was given to Pearse; but Robinson's new left tackle was a good man, and yard by yard Erskine was borne back toward her goal. The south stand blossomed anew with brown silk and bunting.

On her thirty yards Erskine was penalized for off-side and the ball was almost under her goal. The first fierce plunge of the tandem broke the Purple line in twain and the backs went through for three yards. Mason was hurt and the whistle shrilled. A cheer arose from the north stand and a youth running into the field from the side-line heard it with fast-beating heart.

"Erskine! Erskine! Erskine! Rah-rah-rah, rah-rah-rah, rah-rah-rah! Fletcher! Fletcher! Fletcher!"

Mason was taken off, protesting feebly, and on the next plunge of the tackle-tandem Neil, with Pearse behind him, brought hope back to Erskine hearts, for the "antidote" worked to perfection again. All the pent-up strength and enthusiasm of Neil's body and heart were turned loose, and he played, as he had known he could if given the opportunity, as he had never played before, either at Erskine or Hillton. The spirit of battle held him; he was perfectly happy, and every knock and bruise brought him joy rather than pain. His chance had come to prove to both the coaches and the fellows that their first estimate of him was the correct one.

Robinson made her distance and gained the twenty-yard line by a trick play outside of left tackle; but that was all she did on that occasion, for in the next three downs she failed to advance the ball a single inch, and it went to Erskine. Neil dropped back and the pigskin settled into his ready hands. When it next

Ralph Henry Barbour

touched earth it was in Robinson's possession on her own fifty yards. That punt brought a burst of applause from the north seats. Robinson tried tackle-tandem again and Neil and Pearse stopped it short. Again, and again there was no advance; but when Neil picked himself out of the pile-up he made the discovery that something was radically wrong with his right arm and shoulder. He sat down on the trampled turf to think it over and closed his eyes. He heard the whistle and Reardon's voice above him:

"Hurt?"

Neil looked up and shook his head. His gaze fell on Simson headed toward him followed by the water-carrier. He staggered to his feet, Reardon's arm about him.

"Keep 'Baldy' away," he muttered. "I'm all right; but don't let him get to me."

Reardon looked at his white face for a second in doubt. Simson was almost up to them. He wanted to win, did Reardon, and -

"All right here," he cried.

Neil went to his place, Simson retreated, suspicion written all over his face, and the whistle sounded.

Neil met the next attack with his left shoulder fore-most. And it was Erskine's ball on Robinson's fifty-yards.

On the first try around the Brown's left end Smith took the leather twenty yards, catching Bloch napping. The north stand was on its feet in an instant. Cheer after cheer broke forth encouraging the Purple warriors to fight their way across those six remaining white lines and wrest victory from defeat. But there was no time to struggle over the thirty yards that intervened. A long run might bring a touch-down if Erskine could again get a back around an end, but two minutes was too short a time for line-bucking; and, besides, Reardon had his orders.

On the side-line the timekeeper was keeping a careful eye upon his stop-watch.

A try by Neil outside of right tackle netted but a yard and left him half fainting on the ground. Pearse set off for the left end of the line on the next play, but never reached it; the Robinson right tackle got through on to him and stopped him well back of his line.

"Third down," called the referee, "five to gain!"

The teams were lined up about half-way between the Robinson goal and the south side of the field, the ball just inside the thirty-yard line. Reardon had been directed to try for a field-goal as soon as he got inside the twenty-five yards. This was only the thirty yards, and the angle was severe. There was perhaps one chance in three of making a goal from placement; a drop-kick was out of the question. Moreover, to make matters more desperate, Neil was injured; just how badly Reardon didn't know, but the other's white, drawn face told its own story. If the attempt failed he would be held to blame by the coaches, if it succeeded he would be praised for good generalship; it was a way coaches had. His consideration of the problem lasted but a fraction of a minute. He glanced at Neil and their eyes met. The quarter-back's mind was made up on the instant.

"*Signal*!" he cried. "*Steady, fellows; we want this; every one hold hard*!"

He trotted back to the thirty-five-yard line and dropped to his knees, directly behind and almost facing center. Neil took up his position three yards from him and facing the goal. Pearse and Smith stood guard between him and the line. The Robinson right half turned and sped back to join the quarter, whose commands to "Get through and stop this kick!" were being shouted lustily from his position near the goal-line.

"Signal!" Reardon repeated. Graham stooped over the ball. Neil, pale but with a little smile about his mouth, measured his distance. Victory depended upon him. From where Reardon knelt to the goal was nearly forty yards on a straight line and the angle was severe. If he made it, well and good; if he missed - He recalled what Mills had told him ere he sent him in:

"I think you can win this for us, Fletcher. Once inside their twenty-five Reardon will give you the ball for a kick from drop or placement, as you think best. Whatever happens, don't let your nerves get the best of you. If you miss, why, you've missed, that's all. Don't think the world's coming to an end because we've been beaten. A hundred years from now, when you and I aren't even memories, Erskine will still be turning out football teams. But if we can, we want to win. Just keep cool and do your level best, that's all we ask. Now get in there."

Neil took a deep breath. He'd do his best. If the line held, the ball ought to go over. He was cool enough now, and although his shoulder seemed on fire, the smile about his mouth deepened and grew confident. Reardon stretched forth his hands.

"*Signal!*" he cried for the third time; but no signal was forthcoming. Instead Graham sped the ball back to him, steady and true, and the Robinson line, almost caught napping, failed to charge until the oval had settled into Reardon's hands and had been placed upon the ground well cocked at the goal. Then the Brown's warriors broke through and bore down, big and ugly, upon Pearse and Smith; but Neil was stepping toward the ball; a long stride, a short one, a long one, and toe and pigskin came together. Pearse was down and Smith was shouldering valiantly at a big guard. Two blue-clad arms swept upward almost into the path of the rising ball; there was a confused sound of crashing bodies and rasping canvas, and then a Robinson man bounded against Neil and sent him reeling to earth.

For an instant the desire to lie still and close his eyes was strong. But there was the ball! He rolled half over, and raising himself on his left hand looked eagerly toward the posts. The pigskin, turning lazily over and over, was still in flight. Straight for the goal it was speeding, but now it had begun to drop. Neil's heart stood still. Would it clear the cross-bar? It seemed scarcely possible, but even as despair seized him, for an instant the bar came between his straining eyes and the dropping ball!

A figure with tattered purple sleeves near at hand leaped into the air, waving his arms wildly. On the stand across the field pandemonium broke loose.

Neil closed his eyes.

A moment later Simson found him there, sitting on the thirty-five-yard line, one arm hanging limply over his knee, his eyes closed, and his white face wreathed in smiles.

Erskine 10, Opponents 6, said the score-board.

CHAPTER XXIV

AFTER THE BATTLE

"You'll not get off so easily this time," said the doctor.

"No, sir," replied Neil, striving to look concerned.

He was back on the couch again, just where he had been four weeks previous, with his shoulder swathed about in bandages just as it had been then.

"I can't see what you were thinking about," went on the other irritably, "to go on playing after you'd bust things up again."

"No, sir - that is, I'm sure I don't know." Neil's tone was very meek, but the doctor nevertheless looked at him suspiciously.

"Humph! Much you care, I guess. But, just the same, my fine fellow, it'll be Christmas before you have the use of that arm again. That'll give you time to see what an idiot you were."

"Thank you, sir."

The doctor smiled in spite of himself and looked away.

"Doesn't seem to have interfered with your appetite, anyhow," he said, glancing at the well-nigh empty tray on the chair.

"No, sir; I - I tried not to eat much, but I was terribly hungry, Doc."

"Oh, I guess you'll do." He picked up his hat; then he faced the couch again and its occupant. "The trouble with you chaps," he said severely, "is that as long as you've managed to get a silly old leather wind-bag over a fool streak of lime you think it doesn't matter how much you've broke yourselves to pieces."

"Yes, it's very thoughtless of us," murmured Neil with deep contriteness.

"Humph!" growled the doctor. "See you in the morning."

When the door had closed Neil reached toward the tray and with much difficulty buttered a piece of Graham bread, almost the only edible thing left. Then he settled back against the pillows, not without several grimaces as the injured shoulder was moved, and contentedly ate it. He was very well satisfied. To be sure, a month of invalidism was not a pleasing prospect, but things might have been worse. And the end paid for all. Robinson had departed with trailing banners; the coaches and the whole college were happy; Paul was happy; Sydney was happy; he was happy himself. Certainly the bally shoulder - ouch! - hurt at times; but, then one can't have everything one wants. His meditations were interrupted by voices and footsteps outside the front door. He bolted the last morsel of bread and awaited the callers.

These proved to be Paul and Sydney and - Neil stared - Tom Cowan.

"Rah-rah-rah!" shouted Paul, slamming the door. "How are they coming, chum? Here's Burr and Cowan to make polite injuries after your inquiries - I mean inquiries - well, you know what I mean. Tom's been saying all sorts of nice things about your playing, and I think he'd like to shake hands with the foot that kicked that goal."

Neil laughed and put out his hand. Cowan, grinning, took it.

"It was fine, Fletcher," he said with genuine enthusiasm. "And, some way, I knew when I saw you drop back that you were going to put it over. I'd have bet a hundred dollars on it!"

"Thunder, you were more confident than I was!" Neil laughed. "I wouldn't have bet more than thirty cents. Well, Board of Strategy, how did you like the game?"

Sydney shook his head gravely.

"I wouldn't care to go through it again," he answered. "I had all kinds of heart disease before the first half was over, and after that I was in a sort of daze; didn't know really whether it was football or Friday-night lectures."

"You ought to have been at table to-night, chum," said Paul. "We made Rome howl. Mills made a speech, and so did Jones and 'Baldy,' and - oh, every one. It was fine!"

"And they cheered a fellow named Fletcher for nearly five minutes," added Sydney. "And -"

"Hear 'em!" Cowan interrupted. From the direction of the yard came a long volley of cheers for Erskine. Dinner was over and the fellows were ready for the celebration; they were warming up.

"Great times to-night," said Paul happily. "I wish you were going out to the field with us, Neil."

"Maybe I will."

"If you try it I'll strap you down," replied Paul indignantly. "By the way, Mills told me to announce his coming. He's terribly tickled, is Mills, although he doesn't say very much."

"He's still wondering how you went stale before the game and then played the way you did," said Sydney. "However, I didn't say anything." He caught himself up and glanced doubtfully toward Cowan. "I don't know whether it's a secret?" He appealed to Neil, who was frowning across at him.

"What's a secret?" demanded Paul.

"Don't mind me," said Cowan. "It may be a secret, but I guessed it long ago, didn't I, Paul?"

"What in thunder are you all talking about?" asked that youth, staring inquiringly from one to another. Sydney saw that he had touched on forbidden ground and now looked elaborately ignorant.

"Oh, nothing, Paul," answered Neil. "When are you all going out to the field?"

"But there is something," his chum protested warmly. "Now out with it. What is it, Cowan? What did you guess?"

"Why, about Fletcher going stale so that you could get into the game," answered Cowan, apparently ignorant of Neil's wrathful grimaces. "I guessed right away. Why -"

"Oh, shut up, won't you?" Neil entreated. "Don't mind them, Paul; they're crazy. Sydney, you're an ass, if you only knew it."

"But I thought he knew -" began Sydney.

"No, I didn't know," said Paul, quietly, his eyes on Neil's averted face. "I - I must have been blind. It's plain enough now, of course. If I had known I wouldn't have taken the place."

"You're all a set of idiots," muttered Neil.

"I'm sorry I said anything," said Sydney, genuinely distressed.

"I'm glad," said Paul. "I'm such a selfish brute that I can't see half an inch before my nose. Chum, all I've got to say -"

"Shut up," cried Neil. "Listen, fellows, they're marching across the common. Some one help me to the window. I want to see."

Paul strode to his side, and putting an arm under his shoulders lifted him to his feet. Sydney lowered the gas and the four crowded to the window. Across the common, a long dark column in the starlight, tramped all Erskine, and at the head marched the band.

"Gee, what a crowd!" muttered Cowan.

The head of the procession passed through the gate and turned toward the house, and the band struck up 'Neath the Elms of Old Erskine. Hundreds of voices joined in and the slow and stately song thundered up toward the star-sprinkled sky.

Paul's arm was still around his room-mate; its clasp tightened a little.

"Say, chum."

"Well?" muttered Neil.

"Thanks."

"Oh, don't bother me," Neil grumbled. "Let's get out of this; they're stopping."

Sydney had stolen, as noiselessly as one may on crutches, to the chandelier, and suddenly the gas flared up, sending a path of light across the street and revealing the three at the window. Neil, exclaiming and protesting, strove to draw back, but Paul held him fast. From the crowd outside came the deep and long-drawn *A-a-ay!* and grew and spread up the line.

And then the cheering began.

Choose from Thousands of 1stWorldLibrary Classics By

Adolphus WilliamWard
Aesop
Agatha Christie
Alexander Aaronsohn
Alexander Kielland
Alexandre Dumas
Alfred Gatty
Alfred Ollivant
Alice Duer Miller
Alice Turner Curtis
Alice Dunbar
Ambrose Bierce
Amelia E. Barr
Andrew Lang
Andrew McFarland Davis
Anna Sewell
Annie Besant
Annie Hamilton Donnell
Annie Payson Call
Anton Chekhov
Arnold Bennett
Arthur Conan Doyle
Arthur Ransome
Atticus
B. M. Bower
Basil King
Bayard Taylor
Ben Macomber
Booth Tarkington
Bram Stoker
C. Collodi
C. E. Orr
C. M. Ingleby
Carolyn Wells
Catherine Parr Traill
Charles A. Eastman
Charles Dickens
Charles Dudley Warner
Charles Farrar Browne
Charles Ives
Charles Kingsley
Charles Lathrop Pack
Charles Whibley
Charles Willing Beale
Charlotte M. Braeme
Charlotte M.Yonge
Clair W. Hayes
Clarence Day Jr.
Clarence E. Mulford

Clemence Housman
Confucius
Cornelis DeWitt Wilcox
Cyril Burleigh
D. H. Lawrence
Daniel Defoe
David Garnett
Don Carlos Janes
Donald Keyhole
Dorothy Kilner
Dougan Clark
E. Nesbit
E.P.Roe
E. Phillips Oppenheim
Edgar Allan Poe
Edgar Rice Burroughs
Edith Wharton
Edward J. O'Biren
John Cournos
Edwin L. Arnold
Eleanor Atkins
Elizabeth Cleghorn
Gaskell
Elizabeth Von Arnim
Ellem Key
Emily Dickinson
Erasmus W. Jones
Ernie Howard Pie
Ethel Turner
Ethel Watts Mumford
Eugenie Foa
Eugene Wood
Evelyn Everett-Green
Everard Cotes
F. J. Cross
Federick Austin Ogg
Ferdinand Ossendowski
Francis Bacon
Francis Darwin
Frances Hodgson Burnett
Frank Gee Patchin
Frank Harris
Frank Jewett Mather
Frank L. Packard
Frederick Trevor Hill
Frederick Winslow Taylor
Friedrich Kerst
Friedrich Nietzsche
Fyodor Dostoyevsky

Gabrielle E. Jackson
Garrett P. Serviss
Gaston Leroux
George Ade
Geroge Bernard Shaw
George Ebers
George Eliot
George MacDonald
George Orwell
George Tucker
George W. Cable
George Wharton James
Gertrude Atherton
Grace E. King
Grant Allen
Guillermo A. Sherwell
Gulielma Zollinger
Gustav Flaubert
H. A. Cody
H. B. Irving
H. G. Wells
H. H. Munro
H. Irving Hancock
H. Rider Haggard
H. W. C. Davis
Hamilton Wright Mabie
Hans Christian Andersen
Harold Avery
Harold McGrath
Harriet Beecher Stowe
Harry Houidini
Helent Hunt Jackson
Helen Nicolay
Hendy David Thoreau
Henrik Ibsen
Henry Adams
Henry Ford
Henry Frost
Henry James
Henry Jones Ford
Henry Seton Merriman
Henry Wadsworth
Longfellow
Henry W Longfellow
Herbert A. Giles
Herbert N. Casson
Herman Hesse
Homer
Honore De Balzac

Horace Walpole
Horatio Alger, Jr.
Howard Pyle
Howard R. Garis
Hugh Lofting
Hugh Walpole
Humphry Ward
Ian Maclaren
Israel Abrahams
J.G.Austin
J. Henri Fabre
J. M. Barrie
J. Macdonald Oxley
J. S. Knowles
J. Storer Clouston
Jack London
Jacob Abbott
James Allen
James Lane Allen
James Andrews
James Baldwin
James DeMille
James Joyce
James Oliver Curwood
James Oppenheim
James Otis
Jane Austen
Jens Peter Jacobsen
Jerome K. Jerome
John Burroughs
John F. Kennedy
John Gay
John Glasworthy
John Habberton
John Joy Bell
John Milton
John Philip Sousa
Jonathan Swift
Joseph Carey
Joseph Conrad
Joseph Jacobs
Julian Hawthrone
Julies Vernes
Justin Huntly McCarthy
Kakuzo Okakura
Kenneth Grahame
Kate Langley Bosher
L. A. Abbot
L. T. Meade
L. Frank Baum
Laura Lee Hope

Laurence Housman
Leo Tolstoy
Leonid Andreyev
Lewis Carroll
Lilian Bell
Lloyd Osbourne
Louis Tracy
Louisa May Alcott
Lucy Fitch Perkins
Lucy Maud Montgomery
Lydia Miller Middleton
Lyndon Orr
M. H. Adams
Margaret E. Sangster
Margaret Vandercook
Maria Edgeworth
Maria Thompson Daviess
Mariano Azuela
Marion Polk Angellotti
Mark Overton
Mark Twain
Mary Austin
Mary Cole
Mary Rowlandson
Mary Wollstonecraft
Shelley
Max Beerbohm
Myra Kelly
Nathaniel Hawthrone
O. F. Walton
Oscar Wilde
Owen Johnson
P.G.Wodehouse
Paul and Mable Thorn
Paul G. Tomlinson
Paul Severing
Peter B. Kyne
Plato
R. Derby Holmes
R. L. Stevenson
Rabindranath Tagore
Rahul Alvares
Ralph Waldo Emmerson
Rene Descartes
Rex E. Beach
Richard Harding Davis
Richard Jefferies
Robert Barr
Robert Frost
Robert Gordon Anderson
Robert L. Drake

Robert Lansing
Robert Michael Ballantyne
Robert W. Chambers
Rosa Nouchette Carey
Ross Kay
Rudyard Kipling
Samuel B. Allison
Samuel Hopkins Adams
Sarah Bernhardt
Selma Lagerlof
Sherwood Anderson
Sigmund Freud
Standish O'Grady
Stanley Weyman
Stella Benson
Stephen Crane
Stewart Edward White
Stijn Streuvels
Swami Abhedananda
Swami Parmananda
T. S. Ackland
The Princess Der Ling
Thomas A. Janvier
Thomas A Kempis
Thomas Anderton
Thomas Bailey Aldrich
Thomas Bulfinch
Thomas De Quincey
Thomas H. Huxley
Thomas Hardy
Thomas More
Thornton W. Burgess
U. S. Grant
Valentine Williams
Victor Appleton
Virginia Woolf
Walter Scott
Washington Irving
Wilbur Lawton
Wilkie Collins
Willa Cather
Willard F. Baker
William Makepeace
Thackeray
William W. Walter
Winston Churchill
Yei Theodora Ozaki
Young E. Allison
Zane Grey

www.ingramcontent.com/pod-product-compliance
Lightning Source LLC
Chambersburg PA
CBHW020501100426
42813CB00030B/3073/J